Implementing a Gender-Based Arts Program for Juvenile Offenders

Implementing a Gender-Based Arts Program for Juvenile Offenders

Jill Leslie Rosenbaum
Shelley Spivack

ELSEVIER

AMSTERDAM • BOSTON • HEIDELBERG • LONDON
NEW YORK • OXFORD • PARIS • SAN DIEGO
SAN FRANCISCO • SINGAPORE • SYDNEY • TOKYO
Anderson Publishing is an imprint of Elsevier

Anderson Publishing is an imprint of Elsevier
The Boulevard, Langford Lane, Kidlington, Oxford, OX5 1GB, UK
225 Wyman Street, Waltham, MA 02451, USA

First published 2014

Notices
Knowledge and best practice in this field are constantly changing. As new research
and experience broaden our understanding, changes in research methods, professional
practices, or medical treatment may become necessary.

Practitioners and researchers must always rely on their own experience and knowledge
in evaluating and using any information, methods, compounds, or experiments described
herein. In using such information or methods they should be mindful of their own safety
and the safety of others, including parties for whom they have a professional
responsibility.

To the fullest extent of the law, neither the Publisher nor the authors, contributors,
or editors, assume any liability for any injury and/or damage to persons or property
as a matter of products liability, negligence or otherwise, or from any use or operation
of any methods, products, instructions, or ideas contained in the material herein.

British Library Cataloguing-in-Publication Data
A catalogue record for this book is available from the British Library

Library of Congress Cataloging-in-Publication Data
A catalog record for this book is available from the Library of Congress

ISBN: 978-0-323-26502-7

For information on all Anderson publications
visit our website at store.elsevier.com

This book has been manufactured using Print On Demand technology. Each copy
is produced to order and is limited to black ink. The online version of this book
will show color figures where appropriate.

Working together
to grow libraries in
developing countries

www.elsevier.com • www.bookaid.org

This book is dedicated to all of the youth who have participated in the Buckham/GVRC Share Art Project

Jill Leslie Rosenbaum is a Professor of Criminal Justice at California State University, Fullerton. Her teaching and research focuses on the lives of young women in the juvenile justice system. She is currently completing a project which focuses on the experiences of girls and the effects of violence, neighborhood disorganization and family on their lives.

Shelley Spivack is an Attorney/Referee with the Genesee County Family Court and a Lecturer in the Criminal Justice and Women and Gender Studies Programs at UM-Flint. She received her J.D. from Brooklyn Law School and M.A. from UM-Flint. She is the Director of the Buckham/GVRC Share Art Project and is the President of the Referees Association of Michigan.

CONTENTS

ACKNOWLEDGMENTS

While Shelley's idea was the spark that led to the creation of the Buckham/GVRC Share Art Project, it has been the vision, hard work, and dedication of Project Coordinator Steve Hull that has enabled this program to grow over the past three years. Artist instructors Traci Currie, Todd Onweller, J.T. Thigpen, Maria Freeman, and Kendrick Jones, as well as former Buckham executive director Jen Sikora, have given life to the project through their vision, creativity, and perseverance. Interns Jade Bell, Brittany Waterson, Brandon Bertram, Colette Legault-Fields, and Ella Thorp have brought fresh insights into the program and have done the bulk of the work that has made this book possible, including typing, note-taking and research.

Special recognition goes to Genesee Valley Regional Center (GVRC) director Fred Woelmer and Program Manager Steve Kleiner who have helped us in every way possible to make this program a success. Without their help and cooperation, the program could not have taken place. A special thank you also goes to the GVRC staff and supervisors who have worked closely with us and accommodated us in every way possible.

We would like to thank Joycelyn Pollock for giving us the opportunity to share our experiences and Pam Chester and Marissa LaFleur for their assistance. A very special thank you goes to the readers of our early drafts, Allan Axelrad, Justin Scanlon, Jackie Sheldon Sweeney, and Geri Lane who provided invaluable insight and advice.

Since Jill spent much of the last year living out of a suitcase, she would especially like to thank Bob, Carolee, Joe, Michael, Peggy, and the "Courtyard Crew" for filling her "home away from home" with wonderful friends and lots of laughter. At CSU, Fullerton, special thanks to Dean Angela Della Volpe, Division Chair Steve Stambaough, and Stacy Mallicoat who made it possible for me to be in two places at once; without your assistance and support, I could never have been involved with this project. And, finally, Allan and Ali, thanks for your love, support and understanding my endless absences.

Lastly, it is through the generosity of our funders, The Ruth Mott Foundation, The Community Foundation of Greater Flint, The Greater Flint Arts Council, and The Michigan Council on Arts and Cultural Affairs that the Buckham/GVRC Share Art Project has been made possible

Implementing a Gender-Based Arts Program for Juvenile Offenders is the story of the Buckham/GVRC Share Art Project, a program started in Flint, Michigan in the fall of 2011. As many readers know, Flint has achieved worldwide notoriety through the closing of GM plants and a murder rate surpassing that of all other U.S. cities. Yet, despite the boarded-up buildings, closed schools, and burgeoning welfare rolls, the resilience that can be found in the people of Flint is hard to replicate in cities that have seen better times.

I came to Flint, the birthplace of the modern union movement in America, in 1980 as a recent graduate of Brooklyn Law School in New York. A movie, *With Babies and Banners*, the story of the Women's Emergency Brigade during the Sit Down Strike of 1936–37, inspired me to come to Flint and work as a Legal Aid attorney. Over thirty years later, the inspiration of these brave women continues to motivate me to follow their example and make Flint a better place to live for all its citizens.

I've been asked many times how I came up with the idea for the Buckham/GVRC Share Art Project. My answer is a 16-year-old boy named Randy, who was the first juvenile in Genesee County to be automatically tried as an adult on a charge of first degree murder.

In 1988, I was working as a public defender and was assigned to represent Randy who, while with several friends, had shot his best friend's father. While he was awaiting trial, Randy was held at the Genesee Valley Regional Center, Genesee County's short-term juvenile detention center. I met with Randy weekly for over six months. Soon after meeting him, I found out I was his only visitor, as his mother was in Florida and his father had never been a part of his life. When I went to see Randy, we spent most of our time talking about, not his case, but the artwork that he had done that week. Although he had dropped out of school and never had any type of formal art education, Randy spent most of his time in detention drawing. He drew both in and outside of the art class that was part of the detention center's educational program. Drawing was the life preserver that kept him afloat. It was what gave him hope. It allowed him to express himself, to develop a skill, and to become someone other than the first kid in Genesee County to face life imprisonment without parole.

In March of 2011, when I saw a flyer for "Share Art Flint," a grant program sponsored by the Ruth Mott Foundation, I thought about Randy. As a member of the board of directors of Buckham Gallery, an artist-run contemporary art gallery in downtown Flint, I thought about the talent and expertise our membership possessed; and I thought about the kids at the detention center, who, unlike Randy, now had no arts programming. The idea of "Share Art," which would allow our artist members to share their talents and expertise with the kids in detention, seemed natural. While I had initially envisioned solely a Visual Arts program, Buckham's executive director, Jen Sikora, envisioned the impact that Spoken Word Poetry workshops would have on the youth. She approached one of our artist members, Traci Currie, with the idea. Traci immediately embraced the project, developing not only the Spoken Word portion of the project, but later the concept of a program designed specifically for girls in detention.

Although she was not a part of the original team that developed the project, Jill Rosenbaum, a Flint native who now teaches at California State University, Fullerton, and the co-author of this volume, has become an integral part of its development and operation. When Jill first heard of the project in the fall of 2011, she immediately contacted me and began working with us to further develop the project. Her research on girls in the juvenile justice system has proven invaluable in designing and implementing the gender-specific Spoken Word workshops.

The Buckham/GVRC Share Art Project is now in its third year. It has developed into a multi-disciplinary program encompassing professionals in the arts, juvenile justice, and academic communities. Most importantly, it is a program designed to give kids hope, a program that will give these kids an opportunity to look beyond the violence that populates their world. In creating this program, I hope that the spirit of the brave women who inspired me to come to Flint can live on and make our town known for the works of art it generates, not the young bodies killed on our streets.

−Shelley R. Spivack

We are extremely pleased to present this work as one of the first offerings for the Real World Criminology Series. Jill Rosenbaum and Shelley Spivack's description of a shared arts project with teenage offenders is exactly the type of work we had in mind when developing this series. Our goal was to bridge the divide between academics and field professionals by presenting research and/or program evaluations in all areas of criminal justice in a manner that was easily accessible to everyone, both in terms of marketing and in the manner of presentation. This monograph is a perfect representation of the series in that the authors offer a review of literature relevant to female juvenile offenders—specifically, the pathways model that supports gender-responsive programming—and then offers a program description that is consistent with the extant literature.

These authors do not provide a program evaluation in the sense of a control sample and recidivism analysis. Instead, they describe in detail an exciting program that provides youthful offenders a chance to express themselves in a safe environment. The authors' descriptions of the development of the program provide those who are interested in starting similar programs a richly detailed and honest view of how programs evolve in an organic fashion. Careful documentation and detailed descriptions of events allow others to benefit from what these program developers learned over the course of several phases of program development.

The monograph is also noteworthy in the way it utilizes the voices of the girls themselves to illustrate some of the issues that are well known in the juvenile justice and pathways literature. This work should be of great interest to program developers in the field who are looking for innovative approaches for dealing with female offenders, and also academics who are interested in correctional programs, juvenile justice, and/or female offenders. We hope the reader will benefit from the content of this monograph and look for other monographs in the series that may be of interest.

—Joycelyn M. Pollock

CHAPTER 1

Introduction

In the spring of 2011, the Ruth Mott Foundation initiated the Share Art Flint Community Mini-Grants program in order to bring the arts into underserved areas of the Flint community. Seeing the need for an arts program at the local juvenile detention center, members of the Buckham Fine Arts Project, an artist run co-operative gallery and art center located in downtown Flint, partnered with the administration of the Genesee Valley Regional Center (GVRC) to create a 12-week pilot art program for the youth housed at the detention center.

With monthly juried exhibitions featuring artists from around the globe and a diverse schedule of theatrical and musical performance events, Buckham Fine Arts Project, founded in 1984, has established itself as a leader and innovator in the Michigan arts community. Artist members include faculty from area universities and colleges, as well as working artists and performers in a variety of mediums. With the creation of this project, members sought to embody the Share Art concept by bringing their expertise and skills to the youth temporarily detained at GVRC. Buckham members chose GVRC as the site for the project, as there had not been any arts programs in the facility for the last ten years.

GVRC houses males and females ages 10 to 17 who are ordered into secure detention by the courts in Genesee and surrounding counties. It is a short term detention facility that houses youth pending court disposition or placement in a residential setting. The daily population ranges from a low of 30 to a high of 60 and the average length of stay is approximately 21 days. The facility consists of three wings, with two of the wings containing all male populations and one containing both males and females. Offenses for which the youth are detained range from violation of probation on status offenses to first degree murder. According to the GVRC administration, nearly 95% of the youth housed at GVRC are from Genesee County (70% from the city of Flint), with the remainder coming from neighboring counties.

The need for programming for delinquent youth is particularly acute in Genesee County due to the declining socioeconomic status of its residents and the increasing number of households headed by single-parent families. According to the 2010 census, Genesee County had a population of 425,790. The makeup of the population in the county was 72.7% white, 20.5% African American, 3% Hispanic, and the remaining 3.6% were Native American, Asian, or mixed. In 33% of the households there were children under the age of eighteen. In the county, 43% were two-parent households, 17% were female-headed households, and the remaining were non-family households. The median household income was $38,819, with 21% of the population living below the poverty line. The county seat of Genesee County is Flint, Michigan. The 2010 census indicated the population of Flint was 102,434. The makeup was 56.6% African American, 37.4% white, and the remaining 6% were Native American, Hispanic, Asian, or mixed. Of city households, 23% had both parents living in the home, 29% were female-headed and 40.8% were non-families. In Flint, the median household income was $27,049, with 43.4% living below the poverty line. In addition, Flint has the unfortunate distinction of being the city in America with the highest crime rate and has been ranked in the top three for violent crime in cities of 100,000 for the last five years.

This book charts the evolution of the Buckham/GVRC Share Art Project. It begins with the Pilot Project in 2011, and continues through Phase 3, which concluded in April 2013. Because the focus of this volume is on the development and implementation of gender-specific programming, primary emphasis will be given to the development and implementation of the Spoken Word workshops developed for female juvenile offenders by the Project. For this reason, specific descriptions of the Visual Arts program have not been included; however, references to this program will be made for purposes of comparison.

The pilot project, funded by the Ruth Mott Share Art grant program, was designed to include both Visual Art and Spoken Word Poetry workshops for the youth. In order to expose a maximum number of youth to both sets of workshops, they were set up so that each of GVRC's three housing wings would receive four weeks of each program. Two 90-minute Visual Art workshops were held each Tuesday evening, while two 90-minute Spoken Word Poetry workshops were held each Wednesday evening. Approximately six to ten youths participated in each group, with a total of 82 youths taking part in the program over the course of the first twelve weeks. The project concluded on December 2, 2011 with an exhibit and reception at Buckham Gallery, and the publication of a book highlighting the work created during the Spoken Word Poetry workshops. The details of the Spoken Word portion of the program and the changes made during the initial 12 weeks will be discussed in Chapter 3.

After the conclusion of the pilot project, the organizers, using data and information obtained from the first set of sessions, refined the program; and they also submitted a request for funding to establish a gender-specific Spoken Word poetry program for girls and a Visual Arts and Spoken Word poetry program for boys. The Community Foundation of Greater Flint funded this proposal. The initial gender-specific program took place between July and October of 2012. The first eight weeks were entirely Spoken Word, while the second eight weeks combined Spoken Word and Visual Arts. These two eight-week programs will be described in Chapter 4.

The gender-specific Spoken Word program was further refined with the receipt of a private grant that allowed the project to run from January 2013 through March 2013. The changes made during this session (Phase 3) were based on the experiences in the first two sessions and will be discussed in Chapter 5.

Chapter 6 surveys the responses to the program by the youth, criminal justice professionals, artists, and interns who have worked with the project. The final chapter, Chapter 7, contains recommendations and conclusions made over the eighteen-month period that the program was in existence. Throughout the book, excerpts of the writings of the youth and the words of the staff and professionals will be used. The program participants' work will be reproduced exactly as written, grammatical and spelling mistakes unchanged. These are the words and voices of the participants; and as they have been told throughout the program, "Their words are important, their words have power." Thus, their work remains untouched.

CHAPTER 2

Review of the Literature with Collette Legault-Fields
The Need for Gender-Based Programming

Until quite recently, research on female offenders generally has been ignored by criminal justice practitioners. The rates of arrest, seriousness of crimes committed, and number of incarcerations were thought to be unimportant relative to male criminality and did not warrant special attention. This resulted in little consideration given to girls and women in terms of facility design and management, gender appropriate training for staff working within these facilities, or the types of rehabilitation programming available for the female corrections population. Until very recently, there were few resources for addressing the needs of girls at risk or those already involved with the juvenile justice system.

Toward the close of the 20th century, however, greater attention began to be given to females in the juvenile justice system. Media portrayals of "bad girls" and "girls going wild," coupled with a spike in public awareness of youth crime, focused more attention on girls' (mis) behavior (Chesney-Lind & Irwin, 2008). There has been considerable debate over whether or not this attention has been productive. Some scholars are critical of the trend to place more formal controls on girls' behavior. Others believe that it is necessary to spotlight the pressing need for gender-specific research and solutions (Goodkind, 2005; Hubbard & Matthews, 2008; Chesney-Lind & Okamoto, 2008; OJJDP (GSG), 2008, 2010; Strom, Warner, Tichavsky, & Zahn, 2010).

Not only do males continue to outnumber females in the system, their crimes are significantly different in nature. The types of violations that girls are arrested and incarcerated for are less serious, less violent, and more than twice as likely to be status offenses (NCCD Center for Girls and Young Women, 2009). Though the rate of female arrests between 1997 and 2006 has increased, while the rate of boys' arrests has declined over the same period, there is disagreement about the meaning of these numbers. These data led many to believe that girls were becoming increasingly violent, and the response by the juvenile justice system echoed this belief. Many scholars have asserted that practices such as zero tolerance in schools and families turning to police and juvenile justice officials to deal with family conflicts, account for much of the rise in female criminality (Chesney-Lind & Irwin (2008).

Technical violations, minor drug offenses, lack of suitable alternatives, and detention "for their own good" are further reasons that girls have become increasingly involved in the juvenile justice system (Wu, 2010; Chesney-Lind, Morash and Stevens, 2008). However, the rise in minor offenses may actually mask the more serious problems girls are experiencing. Running away from home and other status offenses are major contributors to the increase in girls' delinquency. Studies of female chronic runaways show significant levels of sexual and physical victimization (Feitel et al., 1992; Stiffman, 1989; Welsh et al., 1995). This suggests that many of the offenses they commit result from fleeing more serious problems, some involving illegal behavior by adults. As a result, they become extremely vulnerable and are often the victims of prostitution, survival sex, and drug use. Research on assaults committed by females suggests that these behaviors can be best understood in the context of their families, peer groups, schools, and communities (OJJDP (GSG), 2010, p. 3). The research also suggests that female delinquency is qualitatively and quantitatively different from male delinquency (Odgers, Moretti, and Dikon Reppucci, 2005; Watson & Edelman, 2013). Many theorists now emphasize the importance of "gendered pathways" to delinquency. They believe that pathways to crime are not gender neutral. Girls and young women often follow a pattern that, in comparison to boys, is characterized by earlier and more frequent victimization (physical, emotional and/or sexual abuse or neglect) in the home or by intimates. This, in turn, often causes them to abuse substances, run away, and/or quit school as a form of survival.

Once young women are on their own, they are more likely to be subjected to further victimization and exploitation—often by older men who offer a form of "safe haven"—and resort to "survival crimes" such as theft, drug use/dealing, prostitution, and gang involvement (Bloom & Covington, 1998; Wu, 2010, p. 3). Identifying and understanding the ways that gender shapes both girls' and boys' lives is viewed by many in the field as crucial to implementing effective, theory-based programs to address the needs of youth in the juvenile system (Bloom & Covington, 1998; Bloom et al., 2002; Hubbard & Matthews, 2007; Chesney-Lind et al., 2008; Blanchette & Taylor, 2009; Wu, 2010). Just as girls often follow a different trajectory into the juvenile justice system, they also have different needs than boys once they are in the system. Once young women are "justice-involved," their likelihood for "over-detainment" and returning to detention is significantly greater than for boys (Wu, 2010, pp. 2–3; Quraishi, 2012). Utilizing sound theory and focusing on the realities of the life of girls and young women is important when creating gender-sensitive programs for female offenders (Bloom & Covington, 1998, p. 5).

A key component to creating gender-responsive practices involves acknowledging the traumatic experiences of girls on their pathways to delinquency. An overwhelming number of justice-involved girls report histories of multiple forms of trauma such as abuse, neglect, witnessing violence, incest, rape, death of a parent or parents, and loss of a loved one to incarceration (Chesney-Lind, 2008; Odgers et al., 2005) at a higher rate than boys (Wu, 2010, p. 4; NCCD, 2009, p. 8). Furthermore, when these issues are not adequately addressed, girls are at a greater risk for serious mental health issues such as post-traumatic stress disorder (PTSD), depression, self-mutilation, and other harming behaviors. For example, research based on youth incarcerated with the California Youth Authority demonstrated that 65% of girls had suffered from PTSD at some point in their lives, a rate six times higher than the boys (Wu, 2010, p. 4). Girls often engage in significant levels of drug and alcohol experimentation in an effort to cope with their traumatic life experiences, especially family instability. (Bloom et al., 2002, pp. 794–5). Family instability has a different impact on girls than on boys. Girls are more likely than boys to report using alcohol to cope with living with a single parent, and are more likely to "act out" sexually and/or aggressively against family members as a result of domestic conflict (Odgers et al., 2005; Bloom et al., 2002; Strom et al., 2010). One study showed that divorce is more likely to cause depression in boys and delinquency in girls (Bloom et al., 2002, p. 799).

In addition, girls in the juvenile justice system often have greater physical health needs. Unsurprisingly, many have had ongoing health issues—often as a result of trauma, neglect, or inability to access services—that have not been properly addressed, if at all. Reproductive health and/or pregnancy-related problems are common, but other issues related to unhealthy and unsafe environments affect girls' physical well-being (Watson & Edelman, 2013; Chesney-Lind et al., 2008; Bloom et al., 2002, see page 805 in particular). Likewise, female biological factors and developmental issues need to be taken into consideration (Bloom et al., 2002; OJJDP, 2010). Unfortunately, limited health services are provided to juvenile girls in detention. When available, programs tend to be reactive and respond to high crisis issues, but fail to take a proactive or preventative approach (Bloom, 2007). If girls' physical, mental, and emotional health needs are not met, the baggage that weighs upon them from past traumas is likely to be exacerbated in institutional life (Wu, 2010, p. 7). This may provoke behavior that can place them under stricter regulation or disciplinary action. Such behavior is often construed by staff as "acting out, drama, or lashing out" (NCCD, 2009, p. 8; Wu, 2010). Moreover, research suggests that poorly-developed language, social, and problem-solving skills are common in the female delinquent population, and that maladaptive coping styles can be symptomatic of these deficiencies (Sanger, Maag, and Spilker, 2006; Hubbard & Matthews, 2007).

To treat female delinquents in the same fashion as their male counterparts is ineffective; it fails to get at the heart of why girls engage in delinquent behavior and how the context of their lives informs their choices. Gendered socialization and structural inequalities are a lived reality for the majority of girls in the system. Acknowledging the differences and complexities of their experiences as girls and young women is crucial to implementing a gender-responsive program (Brown Morton, 2007; Bloom et al., 2002). Moreover, programs that use an integrative, cooperative, and holistic approach, foster empowerment, emphasize strengths, employ gender-responsive cognitive-behavioral elements, and build self-esteem, resiliency, and self-efficacy are the most effective at addressing girls' needs (Bloom & Covington, 1998; Matthews & Hubbard, 2008; Matthews & Hubbard, 2007; Blanchette & Taylor, 2009; Bloom et al., 2002; Chesney-Lind et al., 2008).

Bloom, Owen, and Covington (2005) state that gender-responsive "principles and strategies are grounded in three intersecting perspectives: the pathways perspective, relational theory and female development, and trauma and addiction theories" (p. 5). The pathways perspective is based on research indicating that gender shapes the routes by which girls and women become involved in the criminal justice system, as well as the factors that work against them once they are involved in the system. Relational theory and the female development model are interrelated concepts that shed light on "the reasons why women [and girls] commit crimes, the motivations behind their behaviors, how they can change their behavior, and their reintegration into the community" (Bloom et al., 2005, p. 5).

Trauma and addiction theories intersect with the first two perspectives because of the recognition that, for female offenders, trauma, victimization, mental health, and addiction are all interconnected and pervasive. Girls (and women) are particularly vulnerable to being re-traumatized within the criminal justice system due to gender bias that still exists in the system. Gender bias, combined with additional issues such as racism, classism, and heterosexism, can be re-traumatizing (Bloom & Covington, 1998; Wu, 2010; NCCD, 2009; Chesney-Lind, et al., 2008). Thus, theories that address traumatic syndromes and issues of delinquency, such as substance abuse, are highly relevant, providing "the integration and foundation for gender responsiveness in the criminal justice system" (Bloom et al., 2005, p. 5).

An additional and interrelated element that is strongly supported by research is the importance of mentors and appropriate female role models. Females, more so than males, benefit on numerous levels when they develop trusting and caring relationships with adult women who show an interest in their lives, listen to them, and respect their ideas and feelings (Matthews & Hubbard, 2008; Bloom et al., 2002; Bloom & Covington, 1998). Chesney-Lind, et al. (2008) state that:

> Multiple sources agree that what girls want most is "someone to listen to me," "someone to talk to." Program documentation reveals some strategies for giving girls permanence in supportive relationships, but that solutions available to the neediest girls are often impermanent and lack intensity.
> **(Chesney-Lind et al., 2008, p. 171)**

They suggest that making the relationships between personnel members and the young women involved a central tenet of a program can be an important component of its design (Chesney-Lind et al., 2008). Positive role models can also be a source of positive reinforcement (Hubbard & Matthews, 2007).

Chesney-Lind et al. (2008) argue that researchers and practitioners must consider what girls and young women have to say about their needs: "Research that gives girls 'voice' to explain their needs produces crucial evidence of the resources, interventions, and programs they might find useful" (Chesney-Lind et al., 2008, p. 167). Similarly, Hubbard and Matthews (2007) maintain that girls should have "a voice in their treatment" (p. 248), a suggestion echoed in the report from the 2012 National Girls Institute Listening Sessions. In listening to girls' input, practitioners gain valuable insight about the needs of girls.

Essential elements and guidelines to consider:

Bloom and Covington (1998) emphasize that when designing a gender-specific treatment plan for female offenders, structure and content are equally significant. A supportive environment is necessary and should have the following attributes:

- *Safety: The environment is free of physical, emotional, and sexual harassment and spoken and unspoken rules of conduct provide appropriate boundaries. Although it may be impossible for a staff member to guarantee safety in her/his agency or institution, it is imperative that the treatment group itself be a safe place.*
- *Connection: Exchanges among the treatment group facilitator and group members need to feel mutual rather than one-way and authoritarian. Females begin to heal when they sense that a group facilitator wants to understand their experiences, is present with them when they recall painful experiences, allows their stories to affect her, and is not overwhelmed by their stories.*
- *Empowerment: The facilitator needs to model how a woman or girl can use power with and for others, rather than either using power over others or being powerless. It is important to set firm, respectful, and empathic limits and to encourage the group members to believe in and exercise their abilities.*

(Bloom & Covington, 1998, pp. 14–15)

Bloom & Covington (1998) also recommend that a number of elements be considered when developing gender-specific correctional programming and factored into service delivery to women and girls. For instance, gender-specific programs must provide gender-relevant opportunities, and not utilize programs designed for males in a female-only program. Female-only programs must recognize the fact that female needs and issues are very different from those of males and should be addressed in a safe, male-free environment. In addition, these programs should be culturally sensitive and build upon the strengths of women.

2.1 ARTS PROGRAMMING

One of the most promising types of programs for girls involved in the juvenile justice system is arts-based programming:

> *Arts programming has been recognized for many years as an important intervention for work with female juvenile offenders. Descriptive studies, anecdotal accounts, and program evaluations have supported the development and continuation of arts programming in corrections.*
>
> **(Lazarri et al., 2005, p. 171)**

However, there is a paucity of literature and models from which to draw when designing a gender-specific arts-based program. The next section is a review of some of the literature about arts education and arts-based programming for youth in the juvenile justice system.

2.1.1 Arts-Based Programming for Juvenile Offenders

Over the last 25 years, researchers in various disciplines have been studying the effectiveness of arts programming for youth detained in correctional facilities. The results have consistently shown that such programming can be an effective tool for the rehabilitation and reintegration of youth who have come into contact with the juvenile justice system (Ross, Fabiano, and Ross, 1988; Ezell and Levy, 2003; Smeijsters, Kurstjen, and Willemars, 2011). Results have been positive when the art form is visual art, dance, theatre, or poetry. The results have been positive when arts programming is introduced through a formal art therapy milieu and when workshops are conducted by working artists. Involvement in the arts "can primarily serve to reduce impulsiveness, regulate anger, and increase empathy and compliance" (Smeijsters et al., 2011, p. 49), which are all essential factors in the rehabilitation and reintegration into society of detained youth.

In 1998, the Office of Juvenile Justice and Delinquency Prevention (OJJDP) partnered with the National Endowment for the Arts (NEA) to fund programs for a two-year project period in order to "enhance existing arts programs in juvenile detention or corrections facilities" (OJJDP, 1998, p. 1). Citing the work of Ross,

Fabiano, and Ross (1988), Calabrese and Adams (1990), and Hillman (1993), the OJJDP concluded that:

> arts based programs for juvenile offenders are highly empowering and trans-
> forming for the participants. . . .participation in arts programming reduces risk
> factors that cause youth to be more susceptible to problem behaviors and
> crime (e.g. social alienation, school failure, impulsivity) and enhances protec-
> tive factors that reduce the impact of risk factors and enable youth to lead
> productive lives (e.g. by increasing communication skills, conflict management
> techniques, and positive peer associations.)
>
> **(OJJDP 1998, p. 1)**

In response to this initiative, the OJJDP and NEA received 60 applications, and grants were awarded to six programs in five states. A review of the programs, *Arts Programs for Juvenile Offenders in Detention and Corrections: A Guide to Promising Practices* (Hillman, 2004), summarizes the programs funded under the grant, provides guidelines for future programming, and suggests recommendations for common problem areas. While the initiative did not use a uniform evaluation method, the programs were found to reduce disciplinary infractions, improve attendance in alternative education settings, and reduce recidivism upon release. In short-term facilities, such as municipal community detention centers, anecdotal information from staff indicated that the "programs reduce stress and anxiety among detainees who are awaiting court hearings and adjudications", moreover, "the tension of unfamiliar surroundings, peers, and staff is diffused by structured activities which can be both individually expressive yet framed within a coop-erative workshop environment" (Hillman, p. 17). Hillman noted that even if a youth only attended one session, it could open up "interests and talents" (p.18) that had not been recognized previ-ously. This *Guide* also includes a useful discussion of issues such as censorship, security, institutional change, confidentiality, supplies, and the oftentimes adversarial relationship that develops with staff members (Hillman, pp. 26–30). While Hillman concluded that there is no uniform program model, he emphasized that broad-based support within the juvenile justice facility, the courts, and the arts community is essential for the success of a program.

Ezell and Levy (2003) conducted a three-year (1996–1998), multi-method evaluation of an arts program in the state of Washington: "A

Changed World" (ACW). In the ACW project, professional artists, including poets, musicians, sculptors, videographers, and graphic designers conducted workshops that ranged from two weeks to two months with detained youth in various facilities throughout the state. The guiding principles stressed individualized curriculum within a team approach that would adapt to the changing needs of the students, a non-judgmental environment, positive role modeling, a 100% commitment to the student and his/her work, and the nurturance of leadership (Ezell and Levy, 2003, p. 110).

In the first year of the study, Ezell and Levy had youth and facility staff measure changes in self-esteem, peer relations, cultural awareness, and community identity, while the teachers assessed the accomplishment of specific learning goals created for each workshop. In the second and third years of the study, the authors collected data from the youth and artists directly after the workshops, using qualitative and quantitative instruments to measure skill development, attitude, behavior, contribution, self-esteem and confidence, ability to collaborate, and interactions. They also obtained data from correctional facility staff and court records to assess institutional behavior and recidivism rates. As a result of the three-year evaluation, Ezell and Levy concluded:

> ACW had a very positive impact on the youth who participated. Workshop goals were accomplished to a very high degree, concrete vocational skills were acquired, and youth had positive feelings of goal accomplishment. Further, while involved in workshops, youth compliance with institutional rules was high and their behavior was less disruptive (p. 113).

The authors identified four major processes that led to the success of the program: "connecting, expressing, learning, and discovery" (p. 13). Through experiential learning activities the youth were able to "forge deep connections with arts, with their pasts, their emotions, and with each other as they develop and expand their talents and techniques to express their pain, joy, and hope" (Ezell and Levy, 2003, p. 113).

In "The Artists Inside Program," Oesterreich and McNie Flores described a two-year study of an arts education program in a juvenile correctional facility in the Southwest. The program used a multi-disciplinary team of professionals (college instructors and a physician) who, though not working professional artists, had visual arts backgrounds. As "participant researchers," Oestrerreich and McNie Flores approached the study of the program as a type of action-research that informed the curriculum and generated new ideas and improvements from session to session. Participant observation, document analysis, and "art elicitation"—"the young men talked about their art and their artistic process"—were among their methods of inquiry (Oesterreich & McNie Flores, 2009, p. 150).

The authors acknowledge that there is insufficient evidence proving that offering arts education in juvenile detention facilities will result in a significant decrease in youth recidivism or immediate changes in youths' lives. However, they believe that the "strength-based approach" created an opportunity for youth to grow, change, and become accountable through participation in the program. They also began to see new possibilities of who they are and the strengths they possess (Oesterreich & McNie Flores, 2009, pp. 159–160).

Many of the studies of arts programming in juvenile facilities involve art therapy, as opposed to art workshops conducted by professional artists. Persons, in his 2009 study of art therapy programs at the Beaumont Juvenile Correctional Center in Virginia, studied 46 boys between the ages of 16 and 20 years who were housed in Virginia's facility for seriously delinquent boys. Each of the boys received two to ten hours of art therapy per week, both in individual and group settings. Displays of the boys' artwork were held both inside and outside the facility. The responses of the boys, teachers, and staff indicated that the art therapy program helped the boys relieve their levels of stress and boredom, boost their self-confidence, and improved their ability to concentrate and focus (Persons, 2009, pp. 442–443). The ability to concentrate on a painting for hours was particularly noteworthy since most of the boys had been diagnosed with ADHD (Persons, 2009, p. 443). Persons emphasized the importance of the "positive approach and atmosphere in art therapy" where the boys were "encouraged instead of criticized" (p. 445).

Smeijsters, Kil, Kurstjen, Welten, & Willemars (2011) conducted a comprehensive two-year study of art, music, dance, and drama therapy programs in six secure institutions for young offenders in the Netherlands. Their conclusions were similar to the findings by previous researchers, who found that art-based therapies "can primarily serve to reduce impulsiveness, regulate anger, and increase empathy and compliance" (Smeijsters et al., 2011, p. 49). Smeijsters et al. also found that arts therapies offered a "protective situation with strong social support and strong attachment in which a positive attitude to the intervention can develop" (p. 49). In comparing arts therapies with other treatment theories, the authors found that arts therapies work "by not focusing directly on the delinquent behavior but instead working in an experimental play space and focusing on the art process and art product" (p. 49). In this regard "art therapists address a deeper personal level that lies at the basis of disturbances, dynamic risk factors, and delinquent behavior" (Smeijsters et al., 2011, p. 40).

2.1.1.1 Gender-Specific Arts Programs

As noted above, studies and models of gender-specific arts programming are scarce. However, the following examples and analyses do attest to the benefits, as well as the challenges, of addressing the needs of young women in the juvenile justice system through the arts and the artistic process.

Emerson and Shelton (2001) studied the use of the creative arts as an intervention for physically and sexually abused female juvenile offenders in the state of Maryland. Focusing on gendered pathways that lead to delinquency and the "cycle of violence [which] results from child abuse and neglect" (Emerson and Shelton, 2001, p. 181), the authors outlined a new approach involving creative written expression for these female juvenile offenders. The 18-session program addressed psychological (low self-esteem, anger), behavioral (substance abuse, offending), biological (depression, PTSD), and interpersonal (problems with intimacy, revictimization) responses to physical and sexual abuse. It used a three-stage treatment: self-care; acknowledgement, re-examination and conceptualization of the trauma; and reintegration into the community.

The creative arts, including dramatic role playing, were crucial to this process, allowing the young women to "reinterpret situations they previously experienced, changing results imaginatively, to test possibilities" (Emerson and Shelton, 2001, p. 190). The girls supported one another, and found their participation in the program rewarding. The creative arts allowed the girls to "become the active 'I' in their lives, in charge of choices and outcomes, rather than the object of others' possibly abusive actions toward them" (Emerson and Shelton, 2001, p. 190). The program gave them positive coping skills that the program helped to develop, and "help[ed] them to bridge the gap between detention and the outside world" (Emerson and Shelton, 2001, p. 190).

Lazzari, Amundson, and Jackson (2005) studied a gender-specific collaboration between a major regional arts museum and a county detention center in the western United States. The project broadly aimed to "influence the thoughts, feelings, and behaviors" of the detained females through engagement with a professional artist in the production of individual and collaborative artwork, including paintings, sculptures, and poetry, that would be publicly displayed at the museum (Lazzari et al., p. 171). The purpose of the exhibition was to raise awareness about the young women in juvenile detention as well as allow them to experience public recognition for their achievements. The program was designed to facilitate the girls' acquisition of prosocial skills, encourage their reinvestment in their education, enable them to experience both private and public success, and provide them with a chance to contribute to and build support networks with their community. The goal of the program was to reduce short-term and long-term violent behavior.

In the second year of the program, the authors conducted semi-structured interviews with 31 current and former participants (ages 11 to 17) over a three-month period. In addition to determining behavioral outcomes, they sought to discover the value and the meaning the participants themselves derived from the program.

The results of this qualitative assessment underline the value and the positive impact of the multidimensional relationships the young women were able to build with the artist, other participants, the art, their families and communities, and themselves. The structured yet nurturing environment created by the artist in his/her role as instructor and as a positive, empathetic adult role model, was crucial in enabling the young women to "develop, to various degrees, insight through self-discovery that contributes to self-efficacy and thus in some cases, leads to self-reported behavioral changes" (Lazzari et al., p. 176). Furthermore, similar to Emerson and Shelton's findings, for young women offenders, the experience of focusing outside herself, on the art, was as empowering as a "socially acceptable vehicle of self-expression" (Lazzari et al., pp. 176, 178). Both visual arts and poetry were seen as valuable outlets for expressing emotions and anger. Other significant benefits of the arts project reported by the authors, included: improved communication and relational skills, as well as enhanced coping skills; greater confidence in abilities; more positive self-image; pride in achievement; a sense of perspective; and a vision of the future beyond their incarceration. The facility's staff also noted that violent behaviors decreased while the project was in progress.

CHAPTER 3

The Pilot Program

Working with an initial grant from the Ruth Mott Foundation's "Share Art Flint" Program, the staff and board of the Buckham Fine Arts Project partnered with the Foundation and GVRC staff to create an arts workshop program that would give detained youth the opportunity to work one-on-one with established artists in the Flint community. As the average length of confinement within GVRC is approximately three weeks, organizers determined that twice-weekly sessions for a period of four weeks would allow participation by a large number of residents, while at the same time giving the youth a concentrated period of time within which to develop a relationship of trust with the artists.

A rotating schedule was devised so that each of GVRC's three wings held workshops on two evenings per week for a period of four consecutive weeks. In order to facilitate a close working relationship between the artists and the residents, two 90-minute sessions were held on each of the two evenings so that the size of the groups would be limited to between six and ten students at a time.

While the original idea for the Share Art Program envisioned only the graphic arts, the program organizers realized that GVRC's residents needed a program that would give them an outlet for their visual creative expressions *and* enable them to use language as a means of self-expression and communication. The result was a program that paired Visual Arts and Spoken Word Poetry workshops.

The teachers who were selected to participate in the program were all working artists who had previously taught or participated in community youth art projects, but had not previously worked in a secure detention setting. Since the program was not designed to be an "art therapy" program, organizers decided that it would not be necessary for the teachers to have any formal training in art therapy techniques. What was deemed essential in choosing the teachers was an ability to connect with youth and an ability to help them understand and transform concepts into different artistic mediums. A painter, who had previously been the director of a local gallery and had worked with alternative education students, was chosen to present the Visual Arts workshops. The Spoken Word Poetry workshops were jointly led by two local Spoken Word poets. One of the teachers was a faculty member who has taught Spoken Word Poetry classes at the University of Michigan-Flint, and also worked extensively with high school and college students. She partnered with a male poet who had previously been one of her students and who had been very active in numerous youth arts organizations in the Flint area.

Lesson plans never remained static during the sessions. The teachers continuously revised and revamped the workshops to fit the varying needs and abilities of the students. As in the program described by Ezell and Levy (2003), the guiding principles of the program consisted of a team approach that would adapt to the changing needs of the students, provide positive role modeling, and create a non-judgmental environment. This would enable the youth to develop their artistic talent while at the same time expressing their "pain, joy and hope" (Ezell and Levy, 2003). All participants were given a notebook so that they could write or draw outside of the workshop sessions.

3.1 SPOKEN WORD

In the Spoken Word Poetry workshops, the artists challenged the participants to explore their own feelings and helped them use language as a means of self-expression and communication. As defined by one of the instructors:

> Spoken Word is used to encourage and inspire. We speak thoughts to get into our feelings and speak about ourselves to show our true meaning.......Spoken Word, when performed most authentically, or "real," requires an earnestness that no one else can tap into because no one knows your story the way you know your story.

The poets were not only teachers and mentors during these sessions, they were also active participants. They set the pace and tone for the sessions. Each presented a Spoken Word piece, sometimes their own and sometimes by others, and also showed videos relating to the theme of the class. The artists asked questions about the poems and the videos, which required the students to actively listen, creating an atmosphere of sharing and active participation. It also allowed the students to engage their intellect by discussing themes and concepts. After discussing the poetry, the students participated in an active written and spoken word exercise. Themes for the workshops included negative and positive identities, mistakes, and life stories. In the last class of each four-week session students were asked to author their own story, which they shared with the group in forms ranging from short poems to lengthy narratives.

3.2 SEPTEMBER GROUPS

3.2.1 Giving Yourself a Name

The first two groups met in September 2011. The two artists (one male and one female, both African American) met with each group for 90 minutes. Teachers were instructed that the content of material shared with and written by the youth could not contain vulgarity, anything about their crime or anything that might incriminate them, or anything pertaining to drugs. Initially, this created issues for the teachers who believed in the importance of authenticity and wanted the youth to talk about themselves. While the youth were accustomed to these parameters, over time, the teachers also became accustomed to working within them. The first class was devoted to "What made you, YOU," which required the participants to own their past and their present. During this class, youth were asked to name themselves by choosing a word that defines them. Some of the words chosen were: *loyal, my brother's keeper, silly,* and *powerful.* When a boy chose a word that was negative, the teacher asked him to rename himself. This began a dialogue about the power of language; that something as simple as your name can define who you are and reflect what you become. The young men were then asked to write why that word best describes them. One young man wrote:

> *I am my brother's keeper because I am 100% real to my people*
> *The street life is all that I know that is real*
> *My brother and boys are all I got in family*
> *That is I are my Brother's Keeper.*

Another chose the word "Loyal":

> *Loyal to me comes from the hood*
> *I'm loyal to all my dogs from my hood*
> *Your hood your from you set your claim*
> *And the gang that you bang*
> *To be loyal you have to have respect and trust*
> *I have the trust and respect*
> *So you can call me Loyalty.*

The artists closed the class by asking the groups to develop a creed or theme that they would work with for the remaining weeks of the session. The first group's was "Life, Respect, Dreams, Hope, Achieve, Reality, Encourage, Inspire," while the second group's was "Plan, Do the Right Thing, Be Positive, Don't Do the Wrong Thing, Encourage Others, Be a Leader." Their creeds provided the themes they worked with in the remaining weeks.

From the very beginning, it became clear that while the boys responded well to both teachers, they were especially drawn to the male teacher. In fact, at the beginning of the second class, the boys began asking him questions about himself. They wanted to know about his life, what he did, where he went to school, and according to one of the artists, the boys listened intensely to what he said, "drinking in" every word. He told the young men that although they may view him as a "nerd," he came from the same area that they had, had done the same things they had, and talked about his experiences through poetry. He was able to bring both facets of his life together using local terminology. Following this discussion, he performed a poem listing musical artists from different genres that influenced and inspired his work. The group easily connected his poem to their creed. The boys understood his choices and began to discuss the influence of music and art on their own lives.

Prior to the first class, one of the staff members told the teachers that some of the boys read at a lower level than would be expected. In fact, he suggested "You have to dumb-down the information." One of the artists responded by saying, "Let's not jump to conclusions." The male instructor responded by performing a poem that talked about a man who was illiterate, but had the ability to play a sport professionally until he injured himself. Many of the boys related to the poem and began to speak of their own experiences. One particular boy, who had yet to say anything, spoke briefly about being afraid to speak because he feared sounding dumb.

3.2.2 Turning Negatives to Positives

The third week focused on negative identities. The youth were shown an excerpt from a documentary on Richard Pryor. They were then asked to tell the group the negative things they had been called. The words/phrases included: *dangerous, mean, nigger, criminal, no-good,* and *devil*. After creating this list, the importance of naming yourself rather than letting others name you was discussed. This discussion included how to eliminate debasing comments and replace them with positive words that describe who you want to become. The boys were then asked to replace the negative names with positive names. There was a significant difference between the younger and older groups. The older group had no problem identifying positive phrases, but the younger group had a great deal of difficulty. The youth then selected words with positive associations.

Examples included:

Opportunity...to change your life
Respect...taking care of your actions
Memory...thinking, using your mind
Goals...to do what is right and do what you is told
Honesty...telling the truth
Chance...another chance to go home, help my mom and go to school

3.2.3 Telling Your Story

In the final week the first two groups were asked to write their stories. It was made clear to them that no one knows their stories better than they do. They were assured that even if they could not rhyme or forgot some words, they were still their stories, and theirs to tell. The artists reiterated their belief that everyone has an important story to tell. One young man, who had been in foster care for eight years, described the pain he experienced:

Life was very hard since 2003
My life changed when I 8, not 3
I try to find a family if its there
Pain, no love, trying to find somewhere to go
No family, No pride, No world, No love
No friends, just me, myself and I
Trying to live my life where it is
Not lookin back on them years

Another young man wrote the following, entitled "My Life":

My life is complicated
It is full of frustration,
Hate, desperation, joy
Depression, memories,
Inspiration, expectations
It is full of drama
And good sometimes

I often get confused
And block out all positive
Thoughts and release negative thoughts
And everything I touch crumbles

When others began writing, one of the boys just sat and stared at his paper. When asked why, he informed the teacher that he would be "moving from one set of walls to another" and would be there for quite some time. He added, "What's the use?" Yet, during a lull among the participants, he stood up, looked down at the table, and offered his own story of being bullied and bullying. It was a poem/story and he exhibited quiet confidence as he spoke.

3.3 OCTOBER

At the beginning of October 2011, the artists began meeting the males in the second wing, with a better understanding of what to expect. Again, the instructors asked each group to develop their own creed. The creeds were:

You don't have to hold in feelings.
Listen and observe.
Release sadness and happiness by writing.
Tell others about you.

And

Spoken Word is used to encourage and inspire.
We speak thoughts to get into our feelings and speak about ourselves to show our true meaning.
We speak and write about decisions that affect your future.

These were repeated each week. The teachers then discussed the importance of naming themselves, asking each boy to choose a word that he felt described himself. Along with the usual names, *Mean, Bad, Brother,* two stood out. The first was chosen by the youngest in the group who also had a stutter. The word that he chose was "determined." The other youths all acknowledged that the word fit him because he was always determined to finish what he started, whether it was a positive or negative activity. As he stood before the group, reading his work, some of the boys wanted to finish his sentences (a fairly common occurrence). The artists took this opportunity to remind the rest of the group that this was his story, not theirs to tell, and allowed him to continue, regardless of the time it took. Another young man, who had just been detained that day, chose the word "pissed." He was clearly "pissed "that he was there, "pissed" he had gotten caught (and seemed to every time), "pissed" that his friends were out there and he was not, and "pissed" that he couldn't stop getting into trouble.

The young men were asked to write in any way that they felt comfortable about the word they had chosen. Two very different examples of their work follow:

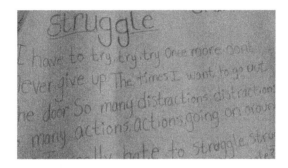

While both young men conveyed what the word meant to them, they did so in very different ways. The artists made sure that they understood that there was no "right" way to write about their word.

3.3.1 Changes
The following week, the teachers tried to channel the boys' anger into something positive. They discussed how being pissed can be a good thing. Then, the male artist had a "brother to brother" talk, which led to a discussion of "running with the wrong crowd." While acknowledging the difficulty in separating from the wrong kind of friends, he

challenged them to write about how they might go about it. The female artist noted that this was when she realized why he always wore a tie to class and made a point of reminding them that he had lived the same life they had. In the following examples, three young men offer their views:

> *I being in jail or dead with baby, Got his mama worried crazy.*
> *Imma get it together and hit the Navy.*

> *I messed up my life trying to hang with the big dogs.*
> *Started smoking at an early age. Now I am all messed up.*
> *I still love my dogs. I don't know what road to pick.*

> *Theres a place I need to go straight ahead is where I show*
> *No more shooting through the crowds, no more walking looking down*
> *No more short cuts, lunch breaks and detours*
> *I refuse to stop until I reach my destination*

Clearly, these writings indicate that these young men recognized the need to make changes in their lives. Through the process of creative writing, they were given the opportunity to think about and develop strategies for implementing such changes.

3.3.2 The Power of Naming

Profiting from their first session experience, the artists showed the young men a Def Poetry Jam performance by Lamont Carey entitled, "I Can't Read" (http://www.youtube.com/watch?v = 1BYDfPOG0LA.) This led to a further discussion of the impact of the names that others give you. The following words were written on the board:

They discussed how hearing the names one is called may lead to people believing those names and acting on them. This included how boys internalize names and act accordingly, sometimes resulting in a stint in detention. Three aspects of personal communication were also discussed:

1. Content—words you speak
2. Body Language—also includes tone and expression
3. Appearance—what you look like

What followed was a discussion of second chances and the desire to prove family, friends, and strangers wrong. The youth were asked: "If others can't/won't see past your mistakes and continue to bombard you with negative names, what are you going to do?" The artists suggested that when they are the recipient of negative names they respond with, "I don't receive that." The youth were encouraged to develop a conscious control of situations in which they were faced with negative names. All of the following sessions continued to examine this topic. One of the youth optimistically wrote:

> *Gonna go home on the 3rd*
> *So I can make mom and dad spread the word*
> *My son, he's doing great*
> *Having no more of those sad depressing debates.*

However, most of the boys seemed to believe that people would not be so forgiving. One young man wrote:

> *I don't resent*
> *That they understand what I meant*
> *When I had change as my intent*
> *And instead let their hopes be dead*
> *Close their eyes, bow their head*
> *Only to be led*
> *To despair and dread*
> *And their enraged pain fed*

The artists made a point of continually emphasizing the importance of naming oneself positively. They began each class by asking the youth to give themselves a name, choosing a word or words that best described them that day. The artists continued to repeat critical phrases:

> *I don't receive your name calling.*
> *I don't receive the wrong you are giving me.*
> *I don't receive your lack of faith in me.*

The artists hoped that with constant repetition, the youth might remember these phrases upon their release.

3.3.3 Dealing with Loss

The boys in these two groups tended to focus a great deal on the loss of people they loved. Because the city of Flint has the highest murder rate in the country (66/100,000), the majority of youth in GVRC have lost a friend or family member to violence. In his poem entitled "RIP to all my dead people," one young man mentioned the recent losses of his cousin, his grandpa, and his homeboy. Another wrote:

> Since my sister died my mind has been going crazy.
> Remember when we always used to laugh,
> And since she died my life changed around
> And I have been going crazy.

In a poem titled "RIP MISSING YOU," the youth wrote:

> When you left I was only 7
> Y did you have to leave
> When I pray
> I wonder why God took you away

Another wrote about the loss of his dad, who is currently incarcerated:

> My life I grew up seeing cocaine, guns and money.
> While I sit in a cell, I think it's like hell but really its not.
> I miss my fam, my dad is gone
> I don't have anyone but my mom.
> My dad is locked up because of what he did

The artists were employing the rudiments of post-modern poetry, which can be seen as a form of confessional theatre, to enable the youth to generate insights into their own lives.

3.3.4 Mistakes

During the final week, the young men were asked to write about their mistakes. They talked about ways to improve themselves. Their stories focused on "**not wanting** to rob anyone," "not wanting to carry guns anymore," "**not wanting** to kill anyone," and "**not wanting** to be like my father." The lack of a father figure or positive male role model was a constant theme throughout these sessions. The young men thought they could learn from their fathers' mistakes. Many indicated that they intended to take care of their family and be a better young man.

Their writing suggested that they were learning to take responsibility for their mistakes and not blame others. For example one boy wrote:

> Looking back on what got me here, a 30 minute high and I'm locked up
> I should have known better...
> If I had used foresight, I wouldn't be here using hindsight
> Sometimes all you need is common sense.

Another wrote:

> A time in my life filled with nothing but mistakes
> Always had the courage, it was just misplaced
> Times were right and times were wrong
> Always had my problems to tag along
> My life ain't nothin but a bad song.

One of the other young men wrote:

> I feel like I should change my life
> Before it gets me killed or hurt
> I want to change
> I don't want to sell drugs or carry guns all my life
> I want to change
> I don't want to live my life like my father
> If I don't change
> I am going end up in prison
> Or six feet in the ground.

In examining the writings during this session, the artists reminded the youth, "Your job is to NOT talk about the NOTS. Your job is to talk about what you want, forget about the NOTS." They encouraged the youth to focus on the positive and use their writing to identify strategies that could be used to change.

3.4 NOVEMBER

In the third and final session, the artists took on a new challenge: working with a mixed gender group. Though they had been warned that the young women would be more difficult to work with and that a mixed gender group might pose problems, they hoped it would work. However, they quickly found out that they were dealing with a very different dynamic. In the first group, there were six young women and three young men; the second group had six females and two males. The initial reaction of one of the artists was that what these youths really wanted was love. They wanted to be listened to and they wanted psychological support. This further confirmed that, as instructors, they were filling multiple roles, including adult, teacher, mother, and artist.

During the first week, the artists became aware of the differences in dealing with males and females. While many of the boys joked, were somewhat hostile, and were reluctant to write down and share their thoughts, the girls, for the most part, could not share enough. At first some of the girls came in with looks as if to say, "I dare you to make me participate." They glared at the artists and exhibited very angry body language. The female artist accepted their challenge, and by the end of the evening all the girls were participating. One young woman was clearly having issues with another youth and other members of the group became involved, attempting to convince her to ignore the person causing the distress. The personality issues that emerged in this first week of the mixed gender sessions had not occurred in the prior two sessions.

In the first week of this session, the female artist began the class with her signature piece, a performance poem written in the late 1990s, "I Dream A World."

> I Dream a World
> Where the world eyes me for my skills
> Not my L.A.C.K. or LACCCCC...
> As in L.ate A.gain C.uz C.apabilities C.an't C.onquer C.hemicals
> ...that's for those who are fighting an addiction and seeking a skillful way out...
> I Dream a World
> Where my issues are issue-less as in
> Less-than-the-average only by default and human order
> Or less than nothing at all since average is of no consequence in my dream place
> We all act upon mere faith as in 1 mustard seed, that's all I really need.
> ...that's for those who feel like there is no hope, but still wishing on a seed...

I Dream a World
Where we are all butterflies
Skipping over the cocoon process
As in no seconds no minutes no hours
Just flying like the wings on my back right now
'Cause that's what I need to do right now
Fore there are time I'm thinking, Lord *please fly fly fly me Awayyyyyy*
…that's for my pissed-off days; we all have had them…at least once in our lives…
I Dream a World
Where in-dig-nation flees from my mind
There's no room for curse because
Language is positive and positive is negative
And negative just keeps being positive
Since there is no such thing as negative in my Dream World
So that means
BITCH means female dog without referring to the straight or gay with a BITCH-yyyy
li'l attitude
…that's for those who are loose with their tongue. Cut it off when you begin to bitch…
UGLY is constructive construction
And I am more free with my language so not to offend
My church folk, students, friends, family, and everyone else I didn't mention when
I act this way, and indeed I do act.this.way
but usually it's every 28 days
UGGGGLYYYY.
…it happens to the best of us womenfolk…
I Dream a World
Where 2 + 2 does not = 4 but rather = 8
As in let's look past the problem to create the solution
What I am saying is
I Dream the same dream that was dreamt before I was a seed
Blossomed into a vine
As in my vision of loveliness
Because that is what you are to me
A Dream
That I Dream
You Dream
We Dream
They Dream
Together
Forever and ever

A world without end
So let it be done.
Àse.
  and
Amen.
By Traci Currie

The instructor was immediately struck by the response of the youth. She realized that these youth had no idea what they were about to experience. When they realized they were hearing from both the voices and bodies of the artists, their response was "like WOAH!" and a lot of "WOWS!" Their body language indicated that they were all "in." She then asked the youths to tell her what they'd heard and discussed their various interpretations. This set the tone for the following sessions. From this point on, this poem was used on the first day of each session.

3.4.1 Giving Yourself a Name

As was the case with the previous two groups, the youth were asked to choose a word that described who they were that day and use other words or drawings to further elaborate. One girl in the second group (with only two boys) chose the word "experience." In the middle of her paper she wrote "experience" and surrounded it with words like, *molestation, trust issues, questioning life, attitude,* and *being gay.* She proceeded to explain to the group that she had been molested as a baby and again later in life. And, although she was working on forgiveness, she still didn't trust people. This was far more personal and intense than anything any of the males had shared in the previous eight weeks.

Another young woman initially chose "doubt" as her word; however, she later changed it to "faith" and proceeded to quote scripture and focus on the positive in her life. Other youth chose words such as *inspiration, desperate, trapped, peace,* and *struggle.* The two males in the second group tended to be very supportive of the six young women, and also much more transparent than most of the other males. As one of the teachers noted, this may have been due to the fact that they were outnumbered. One young man in this group described his mother's drug addiction, as well as his own, and described the struggles that both had endured.

Below are a few additional examples of the youths' work.

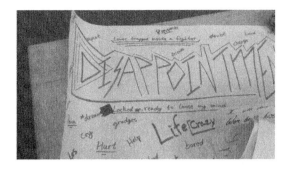

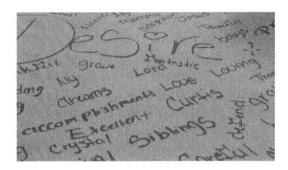

3.4.2 Troubles

The youth were asked to choose a word that would describe a difficulty they had faced and write a poem about that word. The following are examples of their work.

Devastation

All the hate in your soul, you try to describe how you feel
But the feelings are way to real
You're not sure if you want to show
Or if you really want people to know
What will they say?
All the pain you've hid
Since you were a little kid!

Hurt

I'm worth more what you
Putting your love into
Is worth more than 20 bucks
But I'm good I do what I
Do now I have no guidance
I need a mother, a father

But god took him so
What is your excuse?

Trapped
I'm placed in one spot, controlled by many
When I'm out, it's hard to be friendly
It's like I'm in a circle and can't find the exit
Living a hard life, I call that tragic

If the artists were not already convinced that the mixed gender group was problematic, by the end of the second class there was no doubt. It was clear that some of the girls were far more interested in gaining attention from the boys. In fact, a few spent much of the class time flirting with the male teacher. This behavior continued throughout the remainder of the session. The artists tried to get the young women to stay focused and channel their conversations. They chose not to mute their voices; however, they pushed them to think about what they were saying before they said it and tried to get them to focus on the group discussion. They tried to focus everyone on the concept that "words can kill and they can breathe life."

3.4.3 Abuse

One of the artists chose to perform her poem on abuse. Afterward, she realized that the class transitioned to an abuse-release-session, which was not what she had intended, nor was she trained to handle it. As a result, this poem was never used again. During this class, some of the young women wrote about their own abuse and shared what they wrote with the group.

How? Why? Is this really how life goes?
Feeling pain from someone you don't want to touch
Taking away my innocence that I can never get back
I'm never going to be the old me
Its plain to see
Ive let you change me

I say STOP
I say NO
Then I hear a POP
Then I feel a Blow
To my face
My young innocent face
My blood I taste

A little innocent girl no more
You forced on her what she never wanted

You cause destruction
Devastation
I hate you.

Though some of the girls continuously said they would not share their work, over the course of the class, all of them eventually did. While unintended, the session appeared to be a cathartic event for a number of the young women.

3.4.4 Why You are Who You are

The next session was devoted to "who they were and why they were that way." Not surprisingly, many of the youths wrote about what it was like to grow up in Flint. As indicated, Flint has had the unfortunate fate of having the highest murder rate and highest rate of violence in the country for a number of years. The violence these youths have been personally subjected to is almost incomprehensible. In other settings, when this question is posed to students, the focus is generally on their family. As indicated by the following three excerpts, this was not the case for the youth detained in GVRC.

Living in Flint is like living in the jungle
So do what you do but try to stay out of trouble.
People think being smart ain't being cool,
But you can be cool and go to school.

It used to be fight and get knocked down
Now it's run up with your chap you get shot now
Used to be 10 or 15, now its you rot now
It used to be a couple of murders, its been a lot now.
The rate is going up with crime, murders, suicide, homicide, molestation
Everyone is going to end up killing themselves in the middle of all the chaos.

My neighborhood aint game
Everything that happen is truth
Its not just a story
Someone die-they dead
No snitching out
Something real happen
And big numbers hit the fan.

Not surprisingly, growing up surrounded by violence has had a serious emotional impact on these youth. In fact, one young woman said, on a number of occasions, "The streets of Flint are no place for kids."

3.4.5 Telling Your Story

This session concluded in the same manner as the first session and was devoted to writing the youths' own stories. They were reminded that they were their stories to tell and they were the only ones who were able to tell them. In their stories, they shared the raw, hard facts of their difficult lives. For example, one young woman wrote:

> *Self mutilation*
> *A bad reputation*
> *I feel sum agitation*
> *Everyday I'm feeling pain*
> *But I aint changed*
> *I'm still the same*
> *I'm steady walking thru the rain*
> *This just too much, I'm so ashamed.*

Another young woman spoke of her experience being sexually abused and assaulted. In her story she also mentioned that she hoped someday there would be a man who would love her for who she is, not "for what's between her legs."

One young woman used her journal during the week between classes to write her complete life story. In it, she spoke of her parents' addiction to drugs, her own addiction, sexual molestation, and that her only positive male role model was now in prison. The act of writing acted as a catharsis, empowering her to proclaim:

> *I will be a change. Rearrange this life to one better-one that doesn't cause myself and others strife. Learn from my mistakes-Erase the hate. I'm the change-I WILL CHANGE! I control nobody but myself. No one has faith in me, but I will have faith. I will make it through. This is my life I can handle it. This isn't the end. Just the beginning.*

Yet another young woman filled pages describing her father leaving and the aftermath. She spoke of begging her father to stay and give her mother and her one more chance, and even described unpacking the boxes that he had placed by the door. She then described seeing the blood flowing from her mother's wrists upon his departure and how she went to find him and beg once more, only to be denied.

3.4.6 Lessons Learned

The selection of the Spoken Word artists was key to the success of the program. They had a huge influence on the youth. They were both strong African Americans who were part of the community, had finished college, and were individuals the youth could look up to. Many similar programs use people from outside the community. However, these artists were well integrated into the community and understood the issues. As a result, the youth related to them. In addition, the artists understood the importance of serving as adult role models. For some youth, the artists were the first positive adult role models in their lives.

The project staff realized that the failure to take extensive notes and record observations in each session was a mistake. While the artists had specific plans for each session, the response of the youth often required them to change their plan mid-class. Because there was no one systematically recording what was occurring, it was difficult to reconstruct some of the classes. In future programs, it is imperative that an intern or assistant be used for this purpose.

In assessing the program, project staff made significant observations regarding gender issues. Both their observations and the student evaluations pointed out that the Visual Arts workshops had a greater impact upon the male population, while the Spoken Word workshops had a greater impact upon the females. The young women used their notebooks extensively to record their thoughts and feelings, while the boys used the notebooks to create drawings. During the Spoken Word Poetry sessions, many of the boys used both drawings and written words as forms of expression, while the girls appeared to be more comfortable with verbal expression. The girls also appeared to possess a higher level of literacy than the boys, which enabled them to benefit more from the Spoken Word Program.

While the boys often drew during the Spoken Word workshops, the girls often used letters to create "word art" during the Visual Arts sessions. In the surveys completed by the youth, the boys reacted more favorably to skills learned in the Visual Arts workshops, while the girls focused on the collaborative efforts creating murals during these same sessions. In surveys collected from the Spoken Word workshops, the boys expressed positive feelings about the sessions, but generally in one line answers; by contrast, the girls wrote extensively about the ability to open up and express themselves.

The second issue pertaining to gender concerned the inclusion of both males and females in the Spoken Word Poetry workshops. As males and females were both housed within GVRC's North Wing, they received coeducational schooling and programming. While an initial attempt was made to segregate the girls from the boys for the Spoken Word Poetry workshops, uneven population figures prevented this from occurring on a regular basis. Staff noted several issues that arose as a result of integrating males and females in these workshops. Many of the girls housed at GVRC, like the girls in Emerson and Shelton's study (2001), had been the victims of sexual and physical abuse and had experienced gendered pathways leading to delinquency. During the sessions, the recurrent themes involving the young women's prior sexual abuse and other issues related to sexuality and gender identification would surface. The presence of males in the classroom made it difficult to discuss these issues in an open, nurturing, and healing atmosphere. Additionally, the mixing of the sexes in both workshops created sexual tension that at times distracted the students. It was quite obvious to all involved that in the mixed gender group, some of the young women were much more interested in gaining male attention than in what was occurring in class.

CHAPTER 4

Introducing a Gender-Based Program

An analysis of the pilot project led to the development of the second phase of the Buckham/GVRC Share Art Project. As noted in the previous section, gender figured prominently in the conclusions and recommendations by the project organizers.

The need to create gender-based programs for males and females in juvenile detention was further prompted by the fact that the juvenile justice system in Genesee County did not provide any type of gender-specific programming. The Program Director conducted further research, which was used in the design and implementation of the next phase of programming. A grant request was submitted to the Community Foundation, and funding was received for a 16-week, gender-specific program that would include 8 weekly sessions of Spoken Word Poetry workshops for the girls and two sets of 8 weekly sessions for the boys, consisting of both Visual Art and Spoken Word Poetry sessions.[1]

4.1 SPOKEN WORD—GIRLS

Research conducted by Emerson and Shelton (2001), Mullen (1999), and Lazzari, Amundson, and Jackson (2005) on the use of arts-based programming for juvenile and adult female offenders proved crucial in the design of the gender-specific program. In addition, the project organizer reviewed and analyzed the guidelines outlined by Bloom and Covington (1998) regarding programming needs of female juvenile offenders.

The "gendered pathways" to delinquency approach (see Chapter 2), which recognizes the cycle of violence resulting from child abuse and neglect, provided a basis for the development of these workshops. As in the program described by Emerson and Shelton, creative written expression was used to address emotional issues such as low self-esteem,

---

[1] Spoken Word workshops for males were included to determine the validity of the observations of the pilot project concerning the effectiveness of this art form with the male population.

anger, and loss. It would also address behavioral issues, such as substance abuse and issues related to re-offending. The process of writing and speaking gave the young women the ability and opportunity to tell their own stories and thus "become the active 'I' in their lives" (Emerson and Shelton, 2001, p. 190). The all-female workshops provided a safe and non-threatening environment with female role models where the students could address their issues. As noted by Lazzari and colleagues, the relational context, particularly "the young women's relationships with the artist, are central to their experience with the arts project" (Lazzari, et al., 2005, p. 177). Keeping this in mind, project directors chose the female teacher who had taught the Spoken Word workshops during the pilot project to lead this program.

Project directors employed a multidisciplinary approach in creating this phase of the project by consulting with professionals from the arts, criminal justice, and academic communities. In addition to the Spoken Word artist, a graduate student from the University of Michigan-Flint English Department was chosen as the teaching assistant and an intern from the Criminal Justice program at University of Michigan-Flint also participated in the sessions.

As with the pilot project, the transient nature of the population within GVRC proved to be a challenge in developing a program. Unlike residential programs, where a single group of young women participate in the entire 8-week program, the make-up of the group at GVRC changed weekly. While several of the young women were present for a majority of the sessions, others were only present for one or two. Thus, the design of the program needed to allow both continuing and first-time youths to participate and benefit from the workshops. While the artists' approach was flexible to meet the needs of the individual participants, they found that following a specific structural format in each class enabled both the new and returning youth to focus on content and skill development.

The basic workshop format they developed consisted of:

1. Opening with a definition of Spoken Word and a recap of what had taken place in the previous sessions
2. Naming oneself
3. Performance of a spoken word piece by the instructors
4. Responses to each piece by the youth

5. Introduction of the specific theme for the week
6. Writing by the youth on the week's theme
7. Sharing and performance of the youth's writing
8. Discussion of each of the youth's writing
9. Final words or thoughts.

As in the pilot project, the young women were provided with notebooks and were encouraged to write between the sessions.

This particular format developed concrete interpersonal and cognitive skills while allowing for individual expression and creativity. Sessions began with a definition of Spoken Word and a recap of the prior weeks' lessons. This served as a welcoming tool for newcomers, while testing the ability of the returning girls to recall and relate what had previously been covered. It also gave the young women a sense of ownership of the process as they formulated their own definitions of Spoken Word. The process of naming themselves at the start of each session allowed the youth to go outside of their perceived personas. This freed their creativity and provided them with the ability to re-invent themselves during each workshop.

The artists' performances of both original poetry and pieces written by other artists had multiple purposes and effects. While each piece introduced the weekly theme, the performances challenged the young women's abilities to listen and respond to what they had heard. The participants could not be passive listeners. After each piece the instructors would pose the question, "What did you hear?" In addition to improving their cognitive skills, listening to the pieces also triggered empathetic responses from the young women, who connected their own feelings and experiences to the stories of others. Listening to the poetry provided the participants with insight into the lives and emotions of the teachers, forging important bonds between them.

After being challenged to relate what they had heard, the group was transitioned into the weekly theme through the use of participatory exercises requiring the young women to connect what they had heard in the poetry to their own life experiences. The exercises also served as a transition to the writing portion of the workshop by giving the youth an opportunity to develop their own thoughts and ideas.

During the writing portion of the workshop, the young women were provided large sheets of paper and markers to create pieces that related to the specific theme. While they were writing, the instructors and the intern provided assistance when requested. After finishing writing, participants were asked to share their work by reading or performing their pieces. It is important to note that, while they were encouraged to share, the decision to do so remained their own. As with the performance of the poetry by the instructors, the participants were asked after each piece, "What did you hear?" Here, again, while the listening process developed their cognitive skills, their communication skills were enhanced by the conversations that ensued about the pieces.

4.1.1 Telling Your Truth

"Telling Your Truth," the theme of the first workshop, introduced the Project's core concept: "You must be the teller of your own unique story, for if you are silent, others will tell it for you." After defining Spoken Word and naming themselves, the students watched the instructor perform one of her signature pieces: "I Dream a World" (see Chapter 3).

The activity used to transition the girls into writing involved the important concept of self-image. They named five things they liked about their appearance and five things they did not like about their appearance. In this activity, they were more prone to focus on the negative, particularly body image and weight.

The idea of "telling your truth" and becoming the "Active I" in their own lives resonated with the youth. Between the first and second sessions, they all had written extensively in their journals. They wrote about their lives, their loves, and their losses. Some excerpts are as follows:

My life is a reck. It's like I am a train that can't control myself and I'm just crashing into things and I just trying not to crash any more . . .

Look me in my eyes and try to feel my pain. Do you no how It feel to be left out in the rain each and every day . . .

My life is my world
And I love it everyday.
When you see me walk
By I yeah look okay. . .
Trying to make it in this

world without a mother
today. I love her so much
and I miss her til this
Day.

Mom I miss you
with all my harte
I see you face
Every time I talk
I laugh and cry
Every time I say
I love you.

Reading these journal entries helped the instructors understand the depth of the sense of emotional loss experienced by these young women. It also gave them a sense of how disconnected many of them were from the larger world surrounding them.

4.1.2 Naming the Negative—Creating the Positive

Again focusing on the concept of self-image, the theme for the second workshop was "Naming the Negative—Creating the Positive." In this transformative session, the youth wrote down words that affected them negatively. These words were names they had been called by family, friends, strangers, teachers, and even sometimes by themselves. They recorded words like *stupid, nasty*, and *unlovable*, and phrases such as *You will never amount to nothing, you'll be dead before you're 21* and *you're only good for one thing*. After the words and phrases were transposed onto a chalk board, the participants were asked to replace every single negative word or phrase with a positive one. While the young women were quick to supply negative words, creating positive from the negative proved to be a more difficult task. But they persevered and the once seemingly endless list of negatives was transformed into a sea of positives. In this exercise, the words changed, and so did the young women after they realized they had the power to name themselves.

To close the session, several read what they had written in class, while other youth read from their journals. The idea of writing was contagious. Even several new girls, who had not been to the first session, immediately participated by writing in notebooks given to them by GVRC staff.

To keep them writing between sessions, the youth were then asked to choose a word and write a story about that word to present at the next session.

In reflecting on this session, the co-artist wrote:

I'm actually happy that they are all girls in the room because what I have observed over the years is when men are in the room they tend to dominate, and women downplay their abilities or are simply overshadowed. In this room, however, the girls are a lively bunch—full of energy and questions. Despite the circumstances that landed them here, they are beginning to understand that that GVRC can be a place where there is potential for growth. Seeds have been planted.

4.1.3 Life Plans

In week three, the artists focused on the positive formulation of a life plan. Students were asked to state their long-term goals and create a plan to achieve those goals. While the young women all had goals, it was obvious that few had the knowledge or resources to know how to achieve those goals. Their goals and plans included:

Doctor

> *Finish school*
> *Have respect for people*
> *Have an education*
> *Believe in yourself*
> *Positive attitude*
> *Know from right & wrong*

Lawyer

> *You can play b-ball really well*
> *You have skills to be in the WNBA*
> *You'll be a star playing like that*
> *Never give up.*
> *You put up a good argument*

During the first three weeks of the program, the North Wing had been populated solely by females. Between the third and fourth weeks, boys were brought back into the wing. The result was an inevitable change in the dynamic of the session. Although the class remained female only, there was a distinct difference in the attitude of the participants. The group was much more sober than in the previous session and it took them longer to engage in the group process. Additionally, one girl's journal was confiscated for using written profane language.

4.1.4 What Do You Want to Share with the World?

The writing assignment for week four asked, "What do you want to share with the world?" Despite the slow start of the session, it was in this assignment that the young women began to let go and use the creative process to unearth their feelings of loss and anger. One young woman used her writing to help her cope with the recent death of a close friend. She wrote:

> *Heart full of pain*
> *Lost my brother so I'm stuck on one thing*
> *Can't move on so it's hard to make a change*
> *Too busy tryin' to learn the game*

But things still ain't the same
Locked up? I spent a year
It's like my life stuck in reverse gear.

This is a poem for my lil woadie
Jesse my west side homie
I cry at night because of you
When forever ends you'll still be my boo
... I have so many regrets now that you're gone
I should have been there and life feels so wrong
But I now know you're in a better place
And more than anything I miss your face
Just wait my baby we'll meet again
So I'll no longer worry about my lost friend.

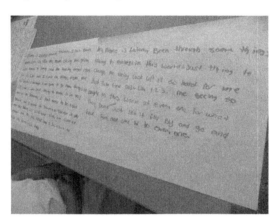

As was seen in the Pilot Program, many of these young women had lost friends and loved ones to violence or accidental death. Their poetry reflected the depth of their loss and how it weighed upon them, oftentimes preventing them from moving ahead with their own lives. Their writing provided them with an outlet and a means to confront their grief. Writing and speaking acted as a catharsis, enabling them to begin the process of healing.

4.1.5 Writing Your Manifesto

Week five brought together the themes from the two prior weeks. The youth were asked to "Write your Manifesto" or "What do you want the world to know about your life plan, goals and a road map to get to these goals?" They also worked on the skill of rhyming. They were told that rhyming affects the tone and presentation of pieces and that rhyming can be used to enhance meaning. One rhyming exercise asked the first young woman to introduce a word and the next tried to rhyme with the word that was given before. This worked well. The youth became so engaged with the exercise that they quickly moved from rhyming words to rhyming sentences.

These exercises showed that the energy and comfort levels of the participants had improved significantly, as had the level of trust between the young women and the teachers. One artist observed, "All of them seemed more comfortable and readily shared. They even asked us for help, which was a change. Trust is being built in this space." The youth used the rhyming exercise to explore how language could express the dual emotions of loss and hope. While some had a difficult time transitioning from the past to the future, others fully embraced the concept of "Writing Your Manifesto."

Two young women chose the phrase "Life is too short" to begin their pieces. One focused on the pain associated with abandonment in her past:

> *Life is too short to take for granted*
> *But the plane went and landed*
> *But I got abandoned*
> *I can't stand it*
> *Sitting here hurting inside*
> *Wondering when it's gonna stop and move on with the pride.*

The second girl wrote a manifesto renouncing drug use, which had led to her detention, and to vocalize her desire to reclaim her future:

> *Life is too short*
> *For me to spend all my time in court*
> *Getting' locked up cuz of bad reports...*
> *Love is too rare*
> *For me to not care*
> *It's like I'm never there*
> *Everyday is a dare*
> *Hate comes too often*
> *Cuz one day I'll be in a coffin*
> *And I hope that day ain't too soon*
> *I have a lot of things I need to fix*
> *I need to stop hittin licks*
> *I'm starting to get sick*
> *Of treating life like a trick.*

Pain from the past and dreams of a brighter future were repeated by many of the young women:

> *You want to hear what I been thru, well let's go*
> *Although I'm trying to hide the pain you got to use steps so,*
> *As I stare at the rain I notice I came from a blessed home*
> *I had the hottest attire so I didn't have to climb step stones*
> *But as I got older, the world grew colder...*
> *But now I wanna make it out and going to start by living it*
> *It all starts with a dream and I won't let nobody limit it*
> *My dream is to find closure and be able to live without the past*
> *I noticed I could be something with no need for greener grass*
> *Maybe find a man to cherish me and make love last*
> *To build a time machine so life won't move too fast.*

A young woman from Flint was awarded the first ever gold medal for women's boxing during the 2012 Summer Olympics. All of the young women were aware of this and some were personally acquainted with her. This not only served as motivation, but was seen as a tangible goal for many of the girls. In the following piece, the writer sees herself as "the knockout queen:"

> *Boxing, yeah that's me*
> *See me in the ring call me knock out queen*
> *I can ball so imagine that scene*
> *Ima step out big money throwing that green*
> *Graduated made it to college so I'm doin my thing*
> *Proud of myself been clean since I was 15*
> *Had pride and faith so I seen my dream...*
> *Steppin to Olympics yeah*
> *Ima get that gold....*

As one of the artists stated, "writing it down and saying it out loud" is the first step in making things happen.

After reciting these powerful pieces, the young women were asked to reflect on their time in detention. The question posed was: "Why is GVRC a blessing?" Responses included learning discipline, getting clean from drugs, and the observation that GVRC was a sanctuary for them, a secure and safe place where they could concentrate on preparing for their future.

By this point in the program, writing in their journals had become a daily routine for some of the youth. While some wrote down thoughts and feelings, others wrote poetry and stories. While issues of loss

continued to dominate, several used the writing process to confront
their drug addiction. Some excerpts are as follows:

> *"My Pain"*
> *There's a lot you can't tell just by looking at*
> *my skin.*
> *So I'm here to share my pain about what*
> *goes on within*
> *On the outside there's a hard shell just*
> *to keep me content*
> *But inside I need a lullabye just*
> *to keep me from the end*
> *I've been hurt mentally and*
> *physically Time and time again*
> *So I don't have time for no*
> *homies, no lovers or no friends. . .*

> *"I love my killer"*
> *people always told me meth is death*
> *well I guess death is my best friend*
> *because for the last nine months of my*
> *life I stayed faithful to it*
> *Faithfully spending all my money on a drug*
> *A drug that kept me up 10 days*
> *A drug that dropped me ten pounds in*
> *two months*
> *A drug that ruined my teeth*
> *Ruined my nose.*
> *Ruined my morals*
> *And destroyed my life.*

> *"How I'm Feeling in side"*
> *I'm sitting hurting inside*
> *wondering when it's gonna stop.*
> *But being locked up don't help it. . .*
> *I lost one*
> *Of my friend on 6-4-12 he got*
> *Shot at Mott Park. I miss*
> *him a lot. . .*
> *Sometime do you ever think about*
> *Crying. Well I do. I cry every night*
> *and think to myself What I do so bad*
> *to make my family to hate me. Sitting*
> *here hurting inside.*

As in prior sessions, the cathartic potential of writing exhibited itself
in the young women's poetry. However, these assignments challenged

them to go beyond describing the feelings of loss, requiring them to examine the roots and causes of their problems and begin thinking about how they could fix them.

4.1.6 How Does Writing Make You Feel?

In week six the instructors built upon the idea of GVRC as a sanctuary where the young women could explore their past and work on determining their own future. Using the theme "How does writing and sharing make you feel?" they were asked to examine how the process of writing affected them individually. This theme was introduced by one of the instructors by reading her own piece, "Why I Write."

At this point, the young women clearly had become engaged in the process of writing and performing. They came into the session announcing that they had written a song that they wanted to perform. Three young women (two from the prior session and one new) got up to perform. The one who had not participated in the prior session was one of the contributors. In addition to the group piece, several others recited poems they had written in their journals during the week. One young woman who had previously written about her meth addiction again reflected on her addiction:

> Withdrawls
> I'm so cold
> but my body's covered in sweat.
> every inch of me aches
> as if I'm painted in bruises head to toe
> Getting out of bed seems impossible
> Like I'm paralyzed
> I wanna scream
> At the top of my lungs
> Until I lose my voice
> I wanna cry...
> But despite all your flaws
> all your hatred
> despite the fact you'll eventually
> kill me
> I'm still gonna pick up the phone
> Call the dope man
> I'm still gonna put you on a plate.

With each passing week, the young women began to write more openly about significant issues that they were confronting. For many of them, writing became cathartic.

Once the writing assignment was announced, they started writing, even the young woman who had her head down during the prior session. While she did not get up to read her piece, she gave it to one of the instructors to read. She wrote that writing makes her feel good, but stated that she trusts no one. Despite her words, the act of asking the instructor to read her paper was a sign of trust. Many vocalized their discovery that the process of writing gave them an opportunity to free themselves of internal and external conflict and the chance to realize their own potential. Examples include:

Writing makes me feel good. It makes me feel like I can let everything out. I feel as if I can say whatever I need without anyone saying anything to me...

When I write I'm confident in that moment like I'm actually good at something. Like my brain and my feelings are back to normal. But sharing my feelings with others makes my heart sink, like the titanic, thousands of below the surface... But I hold back the desire to sit down and I stand up, hoping praying that my words, thoughts, and feelings make someone else wanna stand up and share too.

Writing is like my emotions pouring out of my soul on paper. No one understands until my pen and pad connect. ... Writing expresses that soft sad side people rarely get to see. To watch my words soak in is like music to my ears. Writing is ME.

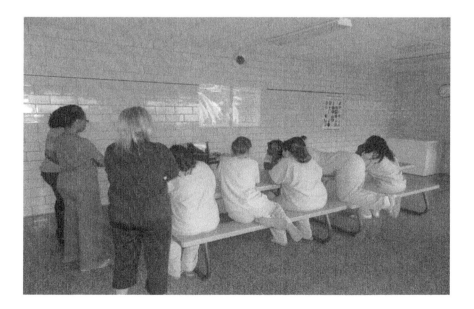

4.1.7 Deconstructing Beauty

It became clear to the instructors that many of the self-esteem issues the young women faced were related to mass media notions of beauty. In response, "Deconstructing Beauty" emerged as the theme for week seven. The session began with one of the instructors sharing a poem about a girl who wanted to change her skin from dark to light because she felt, based on what she had seen on television, lighter skin would make her life better. As the young women talked about the poem, it was clear many of them had experienced similar emotions and thought of themselves as unattractive. The instructors then posed the question: "How and where do you get your image of what beauty looks like?" Their immediate response was that they got it from within themselves, but further exploration of this topic showed the powerful influence mass media had upon all of these young women.

As an exercise, the participants were asked to make a list of famous people they thought were beautiful. Their list included celebrities such as Katie Perry, Beyonce, Alicia Keys, Paris Hilton, and Kim Kardashian. The next question was: "What makes these women beautiful?" They responded with words like *hair, makeup, designer clothes*, and *jewelry*. The list was then expanded to include both older women and full-figured women. Three names were added: Meryl Streep, Jill Scott, and Queen Latifah. When instructors asked them what made those three women beautiful, their answers changed to words like personality and complexion.

The next exercise came back to the original question about where their ideas of beauty originated. They were shown pictures of celebrities before and after makeup was applied and before and after Photoshop/airbrushing. The instructor then asked a new question: "How much different would our lives be if we all took pictures 'as-is' and presented our true selves?" They answered that we would all stop being so negative and would probably have higher self-esteem because we would see that everyone has flaws. They also said they would stop being so quick to judge each other and thought that everyone would be happier. As the discussion continued, the girls explored where their ideas of beauty originated, looking at the media's use of celebrities to sell products such as acne removers. Further discussion then ensued on how the media defines the notion of beauty. The young women appeared to find comfort in realizing that they were really no different than the people they idolize.

The writing assignment for this piece asked the question: "What makes you beautiful?"

During this session, a further breakthrough was made with the young woman who had originally refused to write. She not only wrote, but volunteered to go first, standing up proudly to read what she had written. As each of the young women in turn stood up to tell what made her beautiful, the beauty within each of them radiated throughout the room.

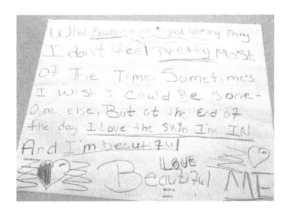

4.1.8 Final Session

As this series of workshops drew to a close with week eight, the young women were asked to write pieces on their favorite things, on change, and on naming. All ten girls shared what they had written on those topics. Knowing it was the last session, the youth wanted their voices to be heard by the instructors, by each other, and most importantly by themselves.

In their list of favorite things, these young women sounded no different than their peers on the outside:

> I have an obsession with shoes!
> I love dance
> My favorite is ballet & hop hop
> My poetry / rapping ability
> My family and caring for them and being able to support them
> Being free and with the people that means the most
> Making people smile
> Candy
> Family
> My boyfriend
> Playing video games
> Shopping

Talking and texting on my phone
My boxing gloves I love it I loose them I would cry

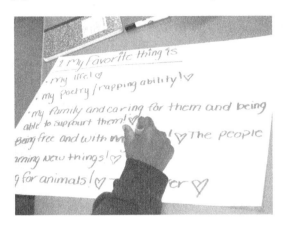

The following poem is an example writing piece about change

Change:
I'll change
I don't know how many times I've said that
I guess I don't try and lie
But what I feel inside don't match up with my words
Because if they did, I'd say
So many things to make addiction go away
And instead of buying meth
I'd do more things to prevent my death. . .
I'd stay out of here
Instead of running away from my tears
I'd be strong
But who knows how long
Until that happens
So I guess I'll just keep saying I'll change
And maybe one day I'll hear my own words

In the final piece of the session, the girls and the instructors recreated themselves through the process of naming:

Why do I call myself Princess:
They call me princess
But my life is far from royal. . .
I make a lot of mistakes like everyone else
And I don't always love myself
But when I hear someone call me Princess
I feel special
Like I have more potential
I don't feel so shy
I never have to lie
Because I'm proud of me

4.2 BOYS PROGRAMMING—FALL 2012

The second phase of the programming under the Community Foundation grant, conducted in fall 2012, consisted of separate Spoken Word and Visual Arts workshops for the boys at GVRC. The results confirmed the conclusions that had been drawn from the pilot project: that the boys responded more favorably to the Visual Arts than to the Spoken Word programming.

Eight Spoken Word workshops were conducted by the male instructor who had co-taught during the pilot project. While the boys' format was similar to the girls, they were generally not engaged in the writing process and group discussions. They were easily distracted and spent much of the time doodling, with their heads on the tables, or provoking other youths in the group. In the majority of the workshop sessions, only a few boys participated in the group discussions and writing exercises. Many of the boys appeared to have significant problems with reading, writing, spelling, and verbal comprehension. When they did write, their vocabularies were extremely limited. Spelling and grammar posed additional problems for them. These deficiencies created a significant barrier to their meaningful participation in this type of program and may have been a reason why some "acted out" instead of listening or participating in the class. It also appeared that the boys were afraid to express their emotions, fearing how the group would respond.

Another factor that may have limited the success of this part of the program was the fact that there was only one instructor, while in both the pilot project and the gender-specific program there were two instructors. More importantly, during the pilot project there was a male and a female instructor. Their different styles of teaching enabled the young men to engage more effectively. The absence of a female instructor in this second series of workshops may have been a factor in the boys' poor response and reticence to express their emotions.

Eight Visual Arts workshops were also conducted by the same instructor who had taught during the pilot project. He worked on both cognitive and physical skills during the lessons. Observations by the intern indicated that the youth remained engaged during the formal exercises and free drawing portions of the sessions. They related well to the instructor, with the tension in the room visibly lessening by the end of each session. It was clear that the boys' self-esteem was enhanced, with them taking pride in the work that they had created.

The drawing skills and memory exercises used by the instructor gave the boys tools to express their feelings and emotions through visual representation. It appeared easier for these boys to express their thoughts and feelings through visual instead of verbal representations. They learned the drawing techniques more easily and were not stymied by problems with reading, writing, and vocabulary. Drawing also allowed them to express themselves without fear of being mocked for their words. They could "say" with a drawing what they could not or would not say with words.

4.2.1 Lessons Learned

This phase of programming generally confirmed the initial findings of the pilot project: (1) That a gender-specific Spoken Word Program was beneficial for the young women; (2) that a Visual Arts program was beneficial for the boys; and (3) that the Spoken Word program the boys received was ineffectual.

The female-only program lessened the sexual tension that was present in the co-ed group. It also allowed the young women to focus on issues that were unique to them, such as self-image, beauty, goals, sexuality, and boys. The male-free environment gave them the freedom to express their thoughts and feelings without the pressure of male judgment. With no boys to distract them, they were better able to concentrate on their writing. The absence of boys also allowed them to showcase their intelligence, which was hidden during the co-ed sessions.

Most importantly, as with the pilot program, the female-only group enhanced the mentoring relationship between the instructors and the group. The young women were more easily able to bond with and relate to the instructors in talking about "girls" issues. They began to see the similarities between themselves and the instructors as women facing many of the same issues. The female-only sessions also gave them an opportunity to have strong professional women role models and work alongside them. The young women felt they were in a safe space and were able to develop a relationship of trust with the instructors and interns.

The choice of Spoken Word as the medium of the gender-specific workshops worked out well. As observed during the pilot project, the young women immediately responded positively to the writing activities. Through verbalizing, both writing and speaking, the young women were given the opportunity to give voice to their issues and concerns. Dialogue between the instructors and the youth, and among the young women themselves, appeared to increase their levels of empathy and decrease tension and hostility in the group. As can be seen in their writings about loss, the creative process channeled feelings of grief that otherwise might have played themselves out in destructive behavior. Writing also gave them an opportunity to confront their own behavior. In writing about addiction and withdrawal, some of the young women took the opportunity to critically examine important issues affecting their lives.

The use of journals also proved beneficial for the young women. Some wrote extensively in their journals during the week between classes, using writing to channel energy and frustration while they remained locked up. The journals also helped them focus on the writing assignments for the following week.

One recommendation for future sessions would be to include time to work on the Spoken Word or verbal aspect of the sessions. While the girls did not hesitate to write, they often had a difficult time presenting what they had written. Additional exercises addressing public speaking skills should be incorporated into future workshops. Time should be set aside in each session for oral presentation of the written work. The artists should work individually with each of the participants to help them speak in front of a group.

While Spoken Word was an appropriate means to introduce the gender-specific program, the young women would also benefit from an introduction to other artistic tools to provide them with even greater means of expression and awareness. Integrating Visual Arts into the program, as well as movement and theatre, could prove productive.

CHAPTER 5

Just the Girls, Winter 2013

Foundation funds were obtained for a 12-week gender-specific Spoken Word program to take place during the winter of 2013. The artists for this phase were the Spoken Word faculty member from the University of Michigan-Flint, who had been with the program since its inception, and one of her former students, who currently works as an Occupational Therapist at a local hospital. In addition to the artists, the staff included the Program Director, Program Administrator, and a student intern. This chapter will focus on the themes addressed throughout the session and the manner in which they were presented.

This third phase built upon the experience from the previous two sessions and utilized the guiding principles of gender-based programming. Paying close attention to the programmatic qualities suggested by Bloom and Covington (1998), the program was "male-free" and focused on concepts relating to safety, connection, and empowerment. In so doing, Phase 3 was approached with certain themes in mind. Rather than trying to introduce a new theme each week, as had been done in the earlier sessions, most of the weekly sessions were devoted to four core themes: the importance of naming yourself, changing directions, response to anger, and identifying dreams and goals. The purpose of focusing on these themes was to give the young women better ways to think about gender and its effect on their lives.

One of the artists introduced Spoken Word to the youth in the following manner:

You will be writing about your feelings and speaking your feelings. You can make it sound like poetry or you can write a story. But the main thing is that this is about you. You are going to talk about yourself, say all of the things that you want the world to know about you. This is your opportunity to tell everyone about you, the things you want people to know about you. You want to define yourself, you are telling the world "This is who I am." You aren't going to let others tell you who you are, that is your job.

As had been the case on the first night of every session, the artist read her signature poem, "I Dream a World," and asked the young women what they heard and what they thought. Their immediate response was that they wanted a copy of the poem, and they received a copy the following week. As one intern noted, "The girls were listening intensely, totally entranced and captured by her words." Some of their comments contained the following observations:

> I like what you said about you trying to be a butterfly, sorta skipping the cocoon process
> She wants the nice stuff
> I like the whole ugly thing every 28 days, because that is the truth
> Your dream world was all positive, no negative
> You always got a positive aspect on things even when they are negative

As had been the case with earlier groups, the discussion then moved to finding an outlet for anger and ways to turn negatives to positives.

5.1 NAMING YOURSELF

As in prior sessions, at the beginning of each class the artists asked the youths to give themselves a name that would define who they were on that evening. Since it is assumed that young women are more likely to internalize demeaning definitions, giving oneself a name is empowering for them and leads to greater resiliency. The instructors used the following exercise to stress the importance of self-definition:

> Tell us who you are. Give yourself a name. That is important because that sets the tone for what we need to talk about. If you want to get out of here, you need to start considering whether or not you want to be a number or a name and who's going to name you. Are you going to let the world name you or are you going to name yourself?

Some of the youths used their actual names, others invented different names. Some changed their name a few times during one 90-minute session, some changed weekly, while others went by their first name. By the final week, all but one of the young women chose to be called by her first name.

The names chosen by the young women included: Tazz, Luck, Louie, Chocolate Drop, Lil Savage, Love, Me, Dreamer, Mother, Mercedes, Thoroughbred, Sky Poo, Flower Bomb, Worlone (Worried Lonely,) and

Miss Strong. The theme of turning negative to positives used in prior phases of programming was again used to remind the young women of the importance of defining themselves and not allowing others to do so. Some of the negative names changed to positive were:

Ignorant	Smart
"Hoe"	Classy
Lazy	Active
Crazy	Controlled
Stupid	Intelligent
Jailbird	Free
Nothing	Something

Over the next few weeks, the young women wrote about who they were and attempted to define who they wanted to be. As evident in the following excerpts, the young women chose to use many of the more positive words that had been discussed in their attempts to define themselves.

Who am I
I am the birds that fly in the sky
I am lovable and neva hurtful
They say I have no feelings
Cause they never see me cry
But deep inside I'm in pain
I am beautiful, I am Briy
I am sexy, I am me
I love my mama
Wish we could drop the drama
I am loyale I told you
Im the truth
I looked hard found nothing
I smoked good weed got caught
Now I am in GVRC

I think about me and everything I've been through
Some say I am crazy, they don't mean that in a bad way
Its more about me doing what I want and sometimes that a bad thing
It sometimes get me sent away to this far away place
Where everything is grey
All I want is to be free and be me

Though many of the girls were initially reluctant to read their work aloud, they were reminded of the importance of their words and their voices. Acknowledging the power of using her own voice, one young woman proclaimed: "My voice is important because it expresses my feelings, a voice from my heart to my mouth." Another wrote:

My voice is important
Because I am inspiration
I am inspiration
Because I have experience
I have learned many lessons
Which resulted in wisdom. . .
Experience has instilled
Intelligence and knowledge
In my head
Insecurities has instilled
Confidence within myself
I am me.

In another session, the young women were asked to choose a word defining how they were feeling that day, to write the word on their paper, and to draw or write about what the feeling would look like. Examples of the illustrations of their feelings included:

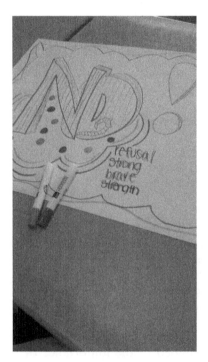

When asked to write further about her word, the young woman who chose the word "NO" wrote:

No home
No family
No feelings
No hope/faith
No money
No friends
No love
No job

Another selected the word "Regret":

Regretful is the opposite of forgetful
When you regret it's hard to forget
It also sometimes makes you upset
Then you always start to fret
So stop regretting and start
Forgetting and maybe it won't be so upsetting

"I don't know" was chosen by another young woman, who began her writing in the following manner:

I don't know how the
Rest of my day is going to be
I don't know if I going to
See another outside world
I don't know if I
Am happy or sad
I'm all around the world right now trying to
Find my way

The second part of this exercise challenged the young women. While it was easy to design and illustrate words, writing about the meaning of the word proved more difficult. Some of the participants sought to change their words, while others dove into the assignment using language as a tool to express and confront their emotions.

5.2 DEALING WITH ANGER AND FORGIVENESS

While staying with the theme "Who am I," the artists added the dimension of dealing with anger. Based on the principles of gender-specific programming, the young women were given writing exercises to help them understand their anger, identify coping skills, and embrace productive, nondestructive behaviors. In one such assignment, the instructors asked the young women to write a "Who am I" letter to themselves. This letter would be written to their "angry self" and they would then explain how their "angry self" would respond. They were told that this was to be a letter to themselves and had nothing to do with anyone else.

> Man you need to give up the Streets.
> you aint Bout that life.
> Man you need to change you to
> Sexy for a Bad lable You got to much
> talent to waste!! Foreal foreal keep
> on Ima Beat yo But in a good
> way. Please change Heart
> You a great Person I Love U Do it
> to Better Yourself think Before your action
> Respect yourself.
> & accomplish all your great goals. Because you no the
> reason you keep getting locked up is your anger. So change
> It. & become the person you no you can be.
>
> Dear Self, Why Are you so Angery? Why Do
> You get all Upset over thangs you have
> No Control over. Why Do You let others
> see your Weakness its okay to feel Angry
> But you have to find other ways to handle your
> self before you End up in a Dangerous situation
> You have to Stop Letting Anger Control you.
> Stop Responsding To Things you cant change
> To Make yourself feel Better Baby you Must
> Learn to Stop Being So Short tempered

We All Make Bad Choices But it Don't
Mean Beat yourself up about it
You Don't have To Be Afarid to show a
Emotion. But.. . . it's about how you control
That Emotion. Stop Trying To use your Anger
for the Reason you use, There are other
Ways to Cope. I' fear for you..
I fear That one Day you will make
The wrong Choice & Something bad will
happen to you. Do you Care weather you
Live you Die? Do you Believe in yourself.
Do You Think You A Failure? Do you wanna
Succed? You Are Worth More Than
That Have faith in yourself Please
Because You Can do It. Repeat After Me I am
Worth More Than That I deserve Better
Than That I am a Worthy human Being

Dear myself,
You tend to get mad a lot, weather its other people
making you upset or you get mad because you
no what you really did was wrong. Or you blame
other people for your mistakes. to make yourself
feel better. I want you to start owning up to what
you do and take responsibilty for your actions. You
can control what you do and how you handle
situations. So try to handle your emotions better.
I know you can do it. (: You also say the reason you
use drugs is to control your emotions weather your
mad or sad, but that's just an excuse, your better than
that turn to something positive,
try other copeing skills I no you can do it,
and be successful in life
& accomplish all your great goals. Because you no the
reason you keep getting locked up is your anger. So change
It. & become the person you no you can be.

When asked to read their letters out loud, all elected to do so. The artists talked about the importance of their letters to themselves and having them serve as their creed. They did not need to remember each and every word or have their paper in front of them when they were released, but they needed to continually remind themselves of their own personal creed.

In another session, which focused on responses to anger, the young women were asked: "When it gets negative and you get upset, what do you do?" The general consensus was that they feed into their negativity, get angry, and their anger leads them to fighting, both verbally and physically. Many identified disrespect by others as the cause of their anger. One of the instructors asked: "If I disrespect you, whose issue is that?" followed by: "If you start fighting me because I disrespected you, who did you give the power to?" While the young women realized that by getting angry they were giving away their control, they were unable to come up with another way of responding. The artists then gave examples of other responses, such as walking away, smiling, and killing with kindness. One young woman said she was going to try saying something like "You look cute when you are angry" or "I am going to pray for you." As a starting point, they were asked to write down different possible responses to being disrespected, rather than becoming angry. The young women were laughing and had fun coming up with clever responses.

As in prior sessions, the participants were asked to identify and explain the emotion they were feeling on that evening. Some of the emotions they identified included: disappointment, being mad, irritated, stuck, calm, and excited.

> My mood right now is mad & disapointed.
> I went to court today and my Judge lectured
> me for a good 20 mins about things Ive already
> heard from him 100 time's. But he really wants
> to send me to placement I got off so easy today.
> Because he kept saying he wants to send me there.
> But Im going to try my best to Stay out of trouble.
> and try not to come back here.
> But Im getting out soon so I can get my life
> on track and do better positive things with my free
> time and take some of the positive things
> I've learned in here with me when I leave
>
> I'm irritated because I got some bad news
> from my p.o. Im getting sent back for awhile
> longer. But I'm not that upset about it. I've
> been here longer then I am now. But today I
> realized that substance abuse is my real problem
> I Just kept thinking about it today & thinking
> I can't wait to get out to do so. But I realized
> thats not the way to go I can't turn to
> negative things when I'm getting irritated. I used

to think thats okay but I really thought about
It today like whats that going to do for me?

I Just need to find other things to do when
I get sad, or irritated because when I really think
about It, Im a really bright intelligent person who
needs different & positive things to do with my time.
I feel Kinda
Stuck. Like there's no
Way to escape the
Guilt I feel for
Putting my family threw
all this crap. But
I feel a little better Becuz
I have Support from My
group And I'm starting to
get over everything.
This Time i came in here
Blaming others, But Yest. i took full
responsiblity for why I am here Theres
Nobody too blame "Nobody" But myself
Because i had the chance To be free.
& i failed To apparantly i didnt
want my freedom that bad. But at
The End of the day I'm Lucky &
Blessed. i've grown Stronger
i no longer Cry Sorrow Tears
I cry Tears of Joy. I was forced
To move out my comfort zone
until somewhere i hate But Thats
Okay, Because i found myself, i also
Learned To Never Judge others
Because you Never Know what they
are going Through. we go through
crumy Things To grow.

The Spoken Word process used in this session had a direct impact on the participants' mood. After writing and reading out loud about their feelings, many of the young women said that they felt better and that the exercise gave them more control over their emotions. The artists talked about training themselves to use writing as a coping skill and how writing could be a good outlet. One of the artists told them:

You need to own your feelings, be truthful and honest about who you are and what you are feeling. If you can stop and write about how you feel, you might be able to come up with a solution while doing so.

They suggested that their journals could be particularly useful for this purpose.

5.3 CHANGING DIRECTIONS

The move to this next theme began with the idea that the young women's time in GVRC was a time to start over. The artists spent a number of weeks talking about changing directions, focusing on defining positive steps that the young women could take once released from GVRC. A number of writing assignments were used to get them to think about who they were and what kind of changes would benefit them. To begin thinking about these issues, one of the artists read the following poem to the group:

> I am here, standing alone, watching you, for the first time,
> Looking and seeing you, desperately seeking, trying to remain
> Relevant, pleading, person to person, like a dance, telling a tale
> About a wolf, never stopping to say, "You, in fact, are the wolf."

The youth were then asked what they'd heard. Some of the responses were:

> You in search of something?
> Whoever that person is, they talking about somebody, but they actually talkin' bout thyself.
> I am seeing you. Kinda like we never met before or something.
> It sounded like you're lookin in the mirror.
> Looking at yourself in a mirror. Like looking for all these things about yourself but like trying to see who you really are, but then you are like the wolf or a bad person or whatever.
> Whoever that person is, they lost. They looking for somethin', but they can't find success, and they running away from something, they desperate to find something, they be hidin.

The artists then asked the young women to think about whether or not they are who they think they are. Because some had difficulty with the concept, they were asked to think about people in their life and identify people who turned out to be different than they originally thought they were. The youth were then asked: "Who do you see when you look at yourself in the mirror?"

These excerpts are the responses of two young women:

> I'm smarter than the things I choose to do.

Not really likin looking at myself right now, but if I look at not just myself but my choices then I like see myself knowing all the right things to say and do, but then I can't.

If I'm lookin across from me, I see somebody that make a lot of wrong choices, but not because they want to but because you know how people just vent

I was young I was good
I meet the wrong people
I made trouble for myself
Went to school walked into
the crowd of trouble
School ended early for me
I thought I was in love[1]
But in all reality I was
Played had A baby And
Decided it was time
For A Change I was
young I was good
I was a young mother
That was misunderstood
I did wrong again.
But am trying to make
Things right I been thru
So much I don't know if
I should turn left or right

Still another wrote about needing to be able to forgive before she could make changes.

Forgiveness is a hard thing to do
I maybe don't want to forgive a person for what he did to me and my family
I been holding onto it, thinking about it and taking it out on someone else.
At times I don't think that person should be forgiven
I've just looked at the bad for a long time.
But I need to learn to forgive
Or I will always be walking around with the anger.

The youth were asked to think about the people who influenced them and identify those who have had a positive influence on them and those who have had a negative influence. The young women could write a poem or just try to identify where people in their life fit on a continuum from most positive to most negative influences. The young women identified far more negative influences than positive and many listed themselves as a negative influence. Sadly, the only positive influence one participant could identify was a female staff member at GVRC. They were then asked to write about whom they would like to have a positive influence on and how they might do so. Most identified a younger sibling, niece, or nephew. One young woman stated that her six-year-old sister looks up to her and that she wants to change so that she can be a better influence. She wrote:

> Whether I notice or not
> I influence the weaker minds around me
> So I do not want people to look at me as trouble
> That influences people to be bad
> I am going to be the person that people go to

In another session, the youth were asked to write a poem about making changes or how they would like to move forward in their life. One young woman wrote about no longer wanting to hurt family members, especially her younger sister:

> I came home drunk one day, literally drunk
> I 'm just falling all over
> I'm zoning in and out
> And then I hear my little sister start to cry
> And she keeps cring "where is my sister?"
> I need to start choosing different things
> I don't want to hurt my little sister like that again

Another wrote about wanting to change so she could be a good influence on her cousin.

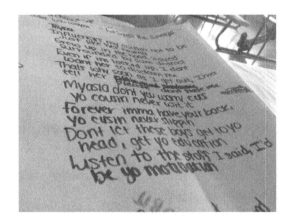

As the theme of "Changing Directions" came to a close, one of the artists told them her story about changing her own life. By the time she was eighteen, she was an addict, had been arrested, and was pregnant. After her son was born, she realized that she needed to change. She changed who she associated with, adjusted her thoughts and direction, went to college, and graduated with honors. She told them how much she loved her current life and her job. But she also told the young women that she wouldn't change any part of where she came from because it made her the tough person that she is today. She acknowledged that for a long time she was stuck and ashamed and, as a result, focused on what she couldn't do. After reminding the young women that everyone gets "stuck in a bad place," she encouraged them to remember her story and focus on the change in direction they want to make. She ended by asking the young women to remember how their own behavior can have a negative influence on those they love and think about what kind of influence they want to be.

5.4 DREAMS AND GOALS

Focusing on defining dreams and goals was identified as a means to talk about positive role models and further define for themselves positive steps that they might take. The artists hoped that once the young women described specific steps that would be necessary to reach their goals, these could serve as their roadmap. The artists asked the young women: "Where do you want to be in about ten years?"

Their initial responses to that question were similar to those in prior sessions:

> *Living*
> *WNBA*
> *Nurse or Paramedic*
> *Cosmetologist*
> *Tattoo Artist*
> *Vet Tech*
> *Makeup Artist*

They were then asked: "How are you going to get there?" Some of their answers were:

> *Graduate High School*
> *Get my GED*
> *Go to College*
> *Get off Probation*
> *Stay off Probation*
> *Stay positive*

The young women were asked their ages. The group's ages ranged from thirteen to sixteen. The artist discussed the fact that things do not happen immediately, so they might want to try to think about reaching their goal by the age of thirty. Rather than become frustrated when things happened slowly, it was important to remember that they had fifteen years to get there and would face many roadblocks along the way. Following a discussion about creating an individual creed, they were asked to write about their dreams and how they were going to get there. This would serve as their own creed, a path for them to follow. The following excerpts reveal some of the young women's goals:

My goals in Life is to
Graduate Next
Year class of 2014. & the following
Year go to Baker or Delta to become
a Register nurse
i also wanna
mentor young girls from ages 12–17.
i also want a
husband & 2 kids a boy & girl.. i want my husband to
Be a christan i want him to have a career
as well. i want him to support the
Things i want to do.... Last But not least
if my mom is still alive i wanna move her
out of Flint into a better home i wanna take
care of her i wanna pay her back & give her
Back all the things i took from her
My Dreams ♥ (: LOVE

My #1 goal in life is to be
a cosmetologist or a theatrical
makeup artist. The very first
thing I have to do is get out of
the court system and get off
of probation. Then I would have
to complete high school successfully.
And I would then, go to cosme-
tology school and learn everything
I need to know. And once I am
ready to look for a job I want
to move to New Jersey and
find an apartment that suits
my style. look for a job at
*a nice salon. *HOPEFULLY* get*

a job! And buy me a teacup
Pomeranian because I don't want
kids. Maybe I would get married. ♥

Another drew a diagram of what her life might include

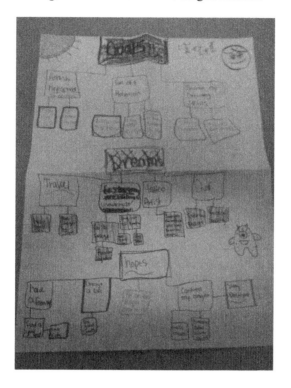

The young women were then asked how they would respond when, upon release from GVRC, someone said to them: "You ain't nothing" or "Why you wanna be that? You're wasting your time." When there was no answer, the artist told them, "You will say 'WATCH ME!' And you are going to remember that you know you need to finish High School and maybe go to college. You are going to believe in yourself, write it, speak it, and have it become your Prophecy." Again, the young women were reminded that they needed to write and speak positively, NOT negatively. The youth were told, "Your job is to NOT talk about the NOTS. Your job is to talk about what you want, forget about the NOTS!"

5.5 LESSONS LEARNED

One of the important lessons learned in this 12-week session was that you never know what impact you have made on the youth. At the beginning of the session, one young woman encouraged some of the other young women to join her in choosing to go to Recreation rather than Spoken Word. The next week they all returned. The ring leader was transferred to a residential facility shortly thereafter. Weeks later, she was returned to GVRC and in her first Spoken Word class, she entered the room wanting to share three poems that she had written about what she had learned from her experiences. She later told the artists that she was planning to read them to the judge at her next court appearance. The artists realized that, much to their surprise, they actually had made an impression on this young woman.

Another important lesson was to keep things simple. It is important to focus on one simple concept per evening. For example, one evening, the young women were asked to think and write about *barriers* they would face upon release. However, many of the participants had no idea what was meant by the term "barriers." This resulted in them becoming reluctant to participate and eventually shutting down.

Using a multi-ethnic, multidisciplinary team is key to a successful program. During the first two phases of the programming, both of the instructors were poets. During Phase 3 one artist, in addition to writing, worked professionally as an occupational therapist. She was able to bring a very different perspective to the program as she was accustomed to helping individuals identify and overcome personal challenges.

Continuity of staff in a program is also an important factor in the success of the program. Since its inception, much of the staff at GVRC and the Arts Program has remained the same. As a result, the GVRC and the Share Art staff have developed a good working relationship. As some GVRC staff acknowledge, they were not "sold on the idea" initially. However, over time, they have become ardent supporters. In fact, the GVRC staff regularly let the artists know what has been going on in the wing that day and what issues may arise.

During the first few weeks of the Winter 2013 session, all journals were taken away from the youth and removed from the facility.

The removal of the journals resulted from two serious incidents of journal misuse. A few of the young women utilized their journals to pass information regarding their charges, a very clear violation of rules. Another youth wrote a poem detailing her crime. According to GVRC staff, about 60 percent of the young women had been using their journals in a productive manner and they were sorry to have to remove the journals. Most of the other 40 percent were not using their journals, and just a few misused them, ruining it for all.

Over the course of this 12-week session, the young women showed an obvious increase in confidence, the development of positive bonds and friendships, and greater support for their peers. Some exemplified empathy and awareness well beyond their years. For example, when one of the participants shared her experiences and emotions regarding being a young teen mom, another wrote a beautiful piece of support, encouragement, and overall compassion in response in less than ten minutes. In another instance, one young woman began assisting another participant, who had difficulty writing, though had much to share.

CHAPTER 6

Response To The Program

Although a means of formal assessment and analysis had not been included within the original grant and program design, by the mid-point of the pilot program, staff decided that a student evaluation should be developed and used throughout the remainder of the program. A short three-question evaluation was created and used at the completion of each of the sessions during the last four weeks. In addition to the written evaluations, the art teachers and several GVRC staff members were interviewed at the completion of the 12-week program.

Three questions were included on the student evaluations:

1. What did you like best about this lesson?
2. What did you find most interesting? Why?
3. Why do you think other young people, like yourself, would want to participate in a lesson?

Overall, the students were very positive about both the Visual Arts and the Spoken Word Poetry workshops. Students surveyed indicated a decrease in stress levels, an increase in their comfort levels around peers, teachers, and staff, an increase in their feelings of self-worth and self-esteem, and a decrease in their feelings of negativity. In both sets of workshops, what the students liked best was the ability to express themselves in a non-judgmental format and the mentoring relationship that developed between the artist-teachers and the students.

In the evaluations from a portrait-drawing workshop, students noted that the lesson taught them to become more observant, to concentrate on multiple things at one time, and to empathize with others. One student's response to the question of what s/he found most interesting was, "Drawing my peer, because as I was drawing, I experienced their feelings." Another commented that the lesson brought the group closer together as they really learned something about one another. The responses from the mural work emphasized the benefit obtained from working together to integrate their individual work into one piece.

In the evaluations from the Spoken Word Poetry workshops, the students emphasized the satisfaction they received from being able to express themselves and talk about their feelings. Comments such as "To know it is ok to express your emotions. Poetry is amazing," and "I don't have to hide anything or worry about being judged" were common throughout all four weeks of the sessions. The sessions also enabled the students to increase their ability to verbalize by putting their thoughts into words.

During Phase 2, another brief questionnaire was given to the students. While the data collected were minimal, a few common themes emerged. When asked if they thought they would continue writing after the class, all but one of the girls said that they would. Their recurring responses were:

> It was a good way of letting out feelings without having to tell anyone
> It is a good way to get stuff out of your mind and don't hurt so much;
> It helps you realize what you have been through and can help you cope;
> I feel like for once someone, somewhere is listening when I write it down.

One young woman stated, "It helps you get your feelings out and relax. You can safely tell a notebook anything." A few of the girls were not as excited because "Writing it down makes me madder" or "I just don't want to think about all of it." On the other hand, while a few of the boys thought that they would continue because "it allows them say what they feel," the majority were just not interested. However, most of the males found the visual arts a better outlet. When asked about whether they would like to attend a similar program when released back into the community, most of the girls said they would like to do so. Those who were not interested cited lack of transportation. Boys were much less interested in continuing the program upon release.

When asked what they liked best about the class, nearly all of the youth, regardless of gender, said the interactions with the teacher. The females also cited learning and writing about Spoken Word, and listening to and talking about other people's poems and stories, as very positive aspects of the program. Furthermore, a number of the young women said that participation in Spoken Word increased their self-confidence. While they were not comfortable speaking in front of people, they did acknowledge that they had improved over time and gained confidence in their ability to do so. The males were far less articulate. They said it was fun and they enjoyed drawing. A few did say that it was one of the few places where they could express their feelings. As with the case in the Spoken Word session, they did not have a lot to say.

The youth were always told that the class was voluntary and that they could choose not to attend or could choose to attend and just listen. Sessions for the girls met during their recreation time, a time when they could socialize with males. One young woman tried to control and dominate during one of the sessions. Once the artists realized the extent to which one young woman can change the energy, they developed different possible plans that could be used depending on the energy on a given evening. The following week, this young woman encouraged part of the group to go to Recreation rather than the Art Session. The artist, informed of the situation, asked the girls who did attend why they had made the decision to attend. The girls' responses were very enlightening. First and foremost, they stated that they "wanted to be around other women" and that the artists showed them "what real women can be." They also acknowledged that they could express their feelings in this setting and even cry, which they could not do in front of the guys. One young woman stated, "I planned on it. I like the poetry. I didn't know I could poetry or anything until this, until now." Another stated that she thought the poetry was "helping her grow as a woman and an individual." After that evening, all of the girls chose to return to class.

While conducting focus groups with the young women for another project throughout the year, the girls were asked about what they thought about their participation in Spoken Word. This came about unintentionally when, during the first focus group shortly after the first Phase 2 session, one of the young women, without being prompted, said, "I liked that we had to write three positive things about ourselves. I had to really think, cos I am just used to thinking about all the bad things people think about me. Now I am trying to remember the positive stuff too." The other focus group members echoed her thoughts. They also emanated pride when talking about the experience, saying things such as, "We caught on quick" and "I had a hard time standing up there talking, but I did it." As a result, in subsequent focus groups, the young women were periodically asked for their thoughts about the program.

During later focus groups, young women noted that they were able to talk about issues that matter to them. One participant stated:

> We get pretty deep into our personal life, if we want. I feel like it helps set aside differences and it helps us relate to things. Cos when you can relate to things, you get a good connection.

Another young woman excitedly offered:

> When we're out, we can think back to spoken word and be like, all right, they were true. Just think about it and be like, all right, don't make that mistake.

And then added, "Now I think I get why we been talking about these things all this time."

Yet another responded by saying:

> I am finding writing to be my freedom. When I'm in here, I hate the weekends. I hate them because you're sitting there thinking about everything you've done and.... When you're in school, you're focused, and you're working, not thinking about the time. You're not thinking about everything else. So, I am trying to focus on writing then. And, when you guys come in, we're actually writing and actually getting feelings down, and that helps too.

One participant from the pilot project, after her release from GVRC, sent a letter and drawings to the Project Director describing the impact the program had upon her:

> ...You may not know this but I'm going to tell you now that you coming to GVRC and running the Spoken Word program truly ment a lot to me... I find you as an inspiration. You allowed me to open up and feel more comfortable speaking of words or about feelings from inside. Your somebody that has it in you to change people's lives + to push people forward + give them motivation- while making adolescents realize life can be worth living and we can make good choices. If nobody's told you thank you lately...Thank you....

However, the most frequent comment was their desire for a similar program once they were released from detention.

6.1 RESPONSE FROM GVRC STAFF

Interviews were conducted with the staff members who had any involvement with the Arts Program. While some were initially skeptical, they all acknowledged that it had had a positive effect on the youth involved and would like to see even more sessions offered at the facility. The staff, as a whole, thought that it was good for the students to have a break from their everyday routine, deal with people they don't know, and have a little fun. More importantly, they had seen changes in the youths' behavior as a result of the program. They noted that, given that females have a greater need to express themselves, they had seen a bigger effect on them than the males. As one staff member stated:

> It's kind of like an antidote for them because they love to express themselves and share their thoughts or feelings any way they can. When they're able to do that a lot of times it take a lot of tension off and it seems as though they just feel more comfortable. For instance, the girls will come back from Spoken Word and I'll have a group meeting with them. That's where we get together and we talk about the problems that happened just from that day. The problems that happened before, they were serious before the meeting, before Spoken Word. Afterwards they're not as bad. It's like, "Yeah, you and I had a problem, but I kind of see your side of it now."

This same theme was reiterated by another staff member who said:

> There have been times where they've gone in there, upset about whatever happened on the wing. There was a lot of anxiety there and then after Spoken Word they're more settled.

Another benefit of Spoken Word that staff identified was increased confidence in the students' ability to express themselves. Many of the young women come in and do not want to talk to anyone. They refuse to address issues in group meeting. However, after participating in Spoken Word, they begin to open up. As one staff member noted:

> You can see that progression where they'll start out very quiet, and you see that through the program where, for example, a recent girl we had, X, very quiet, didn't say a word, didn't talk to anybody. By the last week that she was here, very outspoken, and I think that Spoken Word gave her the ability to express herself, she learned in the safe space of the class that nobody is judging you on what you say.

When the Spoken Word staff declared the gender-based sessions as a "male-free environment," it created some staffing issues at the facility. However, they did comply with the request, even though it required them to change some staff shifts in order to make sure that a female staff member would be available. In addition, the GVRC administrators identified staff members that would not inhibit the youth and made sure that they were available during the sessions. One male administrator stated:

> I think it's much more comfortable for them that it's all females. It is a much better situation. It is the only time that the girls have time in an all-female environment. I realized that it's almost like they don't want to share their secrets with males around.

These decisions created continuity of those involved with the program and, as a result, good relationships among all involved. GVRC staff have become quite open with the Spoken Word staff and make them aware of any issues going on in the ward that might be affecting the young women on any given night. This has, on occasion, resulted in changes to the evening's writing assignment and discussion.

The staff unanimously agreed that it was important for the young women to see strong women in leadership positions. Both the young women and staff all talked about the Spoken Word staff as being great role models for the participants. One GVRC staff member further added that, "Many of these young women have never had a positive female role model." One supervisor acknowledged the importance of having female role models come into the facility because:

> In our society—but especially in the criminal justice system here all the role models are males—males, males, males. When the program came into the facility they got to meet female role model—I guess there's not enough promotion of female role models here.

6.2 RESPONSE OF ARTISTS

The artists were asked to describe how they viewed the program and what they saw as the benefit to the youth. The responses were remarkably similar and are best expressed in the following statement:

> I believe the overall concept of providing these young ladies with a safe space in which to identify and express their ideas and emotions creates the overall foundation for self-actualization and growth. Through writing and speaking exercises, the young ladies were given the opportunity to define who they are, express feelings and identify positive coping strategies for future challenges.

Through writing and Spoken Word exercises, the young ladies identified the importance of self-respect, speaking for themselves, and supporting others when they spoke. Some identified newfound awareness that other people feel the same emotions or have had similar experiences to theirs. For example, when one young woman spoke of her experience with bullying, most of the young ladies in the room quickly supported her and identified with her experience. The response of this young woman was one of disbelief. She had never realized that others had experienced anything similar and explained that she believed that only overweight women, like herself, were victimized in that manner. Furthermore, a number of the adults in the room shared similar experiences. This young woman had been in and out of the system for a number of years, and this was the first time that she realized that she was not alone in her experiences.

The development of a "safe" place was of utmost importance to the artists. One of the artists stated:

> What I think some of the young women took from the session is the opportunity to share their story without hesitation. There were quite a few who worked hard at wanting to find an outlet and safe space for themselves so when they leave GVRC they can return to that "safe space" from within.

The youth knew that what they wrote and shared would not be judged and it was a chance to reflect without recrimination. The "safety of the space" was readily apparent to the young women. For example, one week a young woman who had been processed into GVRC just before the class began, sat through the majority of the class visibly crying, arms crossed, head down, and seemingly unengaged with her peers. That week the young women were asked to write a piece that identified what emotion they were currently feeling. Some of the long-term participants had difficulty with this, but the young woman in tears began writing immediately and quickly filled an entire page of almost poster-board-sized paper. Upon completion of her writing, the young woman was visibly more relaxed and actively engaging in light conversation with her peers. At the end of the 90-minute session, this young woman voluntarily stood up and shared her writing with the class. Following class, the GVCR staff member present explained the young woman's situation, described how shocked she was by the response of this participant, and praised the artists.

The artists recognized that they could only do so much in their limited time. However, they took note of the small changes in the girls' attitudes, demeanor, and confidence. As one artist stated:

> We watched other ladies progress in confidence throughout the program, develop positive bonds and friendships and demonstrated consistent positive support and reactions for their peers.

They took their roles as teacher and adult role model seriously and recognized that the strength of the relationships developed were important to the youth. Their attitude and approach to the limited amount of change they could effect was similar to those of Salzman (2004) who notes in his book *True Notebooks*:

> ...they (youth) responded to encouragement and they wrote honestly; surely that sort of interaction between teacher and student has value, even if it does not lead to success beyond the classroom (p. 322).

6.3 RESPONSE FROM CRIMINAL JUSTICE COMMUNITY

During the course of the program, a number of criminal justice professionals who had contact with the program or the participants were interviewed in order to ascertain their assessment of the impact of this program on the youth. Those interviewed had only positive things to say about the program. They thought it should be continued, and they wanted to see it expanded. Many spoke of the effect of the program on the youth's ability to express themselves. For instance, one Referee stated:

> When I first learned of the Arts in Detention program, I was intrigued. Then, when I saw the results, I was truly moved. Juveniles, who may not otherwise be able or willing to express themselves, freely share their innermost fears and dreams in the universal language that is art. The results are often profound.

A psychologist, who has worked with some of the youth, spoke of the importance of learning how to channel emotions in a positive manner:

> I think young girls, when they really find out what they can do and that they can write and journal, or write poetry, I think they, it opens them up to a whole way to reflect upon what they're doing, and what they're doing in

relationship to others and their community. This program has provided these girls with some real opportunities to express, not only to express to others, but they kind of can reflect back on what they've written. I have nothing, but positive things to say about it.

According to one Probation Officer:

Girls are much more verbal and emotional. Spoken Word is a great way for them to get out their feelings in a healthy way, and not vent it inappropriately. We constantly tell kids, "Use your coping skills," and many of the girls are now using writing as their major coping skills.

One of the unanticipated outcomes was that, once released from detention, some of the girls took their poetry to their court appearances and read their writing to the judge in open court. This was completely unexpected by all of those involved in the case. One judge responded by saying:

Well, I didn't know it was going to happen, and it just completely blew me away, that—I mean, you hope you're doing it. You hope they are understanding. You hope they see it. She got up and read this, and it was her own dialect, and it was her own language, and it was right on. It was right on. We all looked at each other and went, "Okay. Okay, this works."

A psychologist who watched these girls respond in the courtroom after taking part in the program noted:

Knowing who these girls are and having watched them, that, and usually that they're standing there very guarded and they don't say much of anything, that they, the fact that they had done this was really striking to me.

A Referee who has had girls bring their work before him, said:

As a Referee with an interest in art there is also a benefit to me. The art created by the juveniles provides direct insight into how they see the world, the impediments to their success and the obstacles they must overcome. It connects me to them and their world. If I listen to what they are saying, either spoken or visually, I have greater insight and can make better decisions in the hearing room.

In addition, he stated:

They have the opportunity to mentally remove themselves from the negativity that brought them Into the court system, and they instead focus on *something positive that they can control. The act of sharing one's art can be a profound experience. They see that their art, a manifestation of themselves, is appreciated. Positive feedback has the immediate effect of reducing anger and depression, and increasing self-confidence and self-esteem. This is an important step, and helps with rehabilitation and reintegration of juveniles.*

Aside from unanimously praising the program, they all acknowledged that it was unfortunate that the program was not available to the youth upon their release from GVRC. One of the Probation Officers described the situation of one young woman, who had spent a number of months at GVRC, after she was released:

Yeah, she was released from GVRC; this is probably about a month ago. Her first session back after she was released she read a poem that she was still working on. Then the next time she reported to my office the following week—Steve from Spoken Word had dropped off a Maya Angelou book for her, which she was over the moon about.

Then I had one in my library that I gave her too. She was really excited about that. She's a girl who really needs to kind of talk her way through things. She was really proud of her work, and of course we praised her and made a big fuss. I think for that time, although it was kind of short lived, it was pretty powerful. Had she been able to continue in that— like the next day could have gone to a group, maybe we could have kept the ball rolling. But it just sort of fizzled after a point.

And a Mental Health Court Judge told us:

I would love it if Spoken Word went beyond GVRC. I've had girls connect to it, and then they are unable to continue it, have requested it, but unable to continue it. I hate that there's a program available only in a lock up situation; that they can't access as a reward on the outside.

Furthermore, the program staff believed that, because the girls were so engaged and were so willing to show up, the program would definitely be enhanced if it were continued outside of GVRC. Continuing the program on the outside would provide these young women with an affirmative and consistent place for positive support from their peers and from mentors in the community. How this might be achieved was described by one staff member:

I would like to see it as a reward, as a diversion, as something that they can leave, let it be GVRC or an alternative while they're in probation to come into a gender-based program and say to them, "You get one chance. If you're here, you do well, we'll work with you." We can even report back to their probation officer, to their caseworker, to whatever, that they're interacting. If they re-offend or if they're detained again, that would be the end of it.

In one focus group, when asked what they thought would be helpful to them and other young women in the community, one girl stated: "You know that Spoken Word that comes here? Well, I think we should have it on the out. It makes us think about the right things." The girls in the group unanimously agreed.

6.4 INTERN'S RESPONSE

Interns were brought into the program from its inception. Their roles were based on their abilities and their comfort levels. Some were very comfortable interacting with the youth and sharing their own writings with them, others were responsible for making sure that the room was set up with all supplies needed for that evening and as observers/notetakers. Regardless of their roles, all of the interns were included in all planning and recap discussions. Thus, unlike most internship experiences, these interns were team members who not only witnessed the intensity of the classes, but also all of the work that went into each week's session. All responded positively to the experience, and some continued on long after their internship was completed. The following is part of a letter written to the Program Director by Brittany Waterson one of the student interns:

I didn't grow up "wealthy" in the way that most people use the term "wealth." I wasn't handed the keys to a brand new car at age 16. I never carried the latest and greatest handbag or cell phone. I wasn't sent to Cancun for senior-year spring break. Before participating in the spoken word program at GVRC, these are the types of luxuries I associated with the word "wealthy."

I used to envy young adults, whose parents fed their bank accounts on a monthly basis; people who lived worry-free, never knowing what it felt like to have the responsibility of work and bills. These were my biggest burdens and complaints. How pathetic.

To this day, I don't know what exactly prompted my participation in the GVRC program. I suppose it was primarily out of curiosity. I was also coming to the end of my time as a criminal justice major and knew an 8-week stint at the detention center was probably the closest I'd ever come to working in the field. And so, I signed on.

I expected to be greeted with hardened, angry, thug-like faces and equally intimidating attitudes. I imagined young, shackled, women spewing vile language and possible violence. When the girls walked into the cafeteria-type room, I was shocked. Not because they were out of control or behaving like caged convicts, but because they were merely that: young girls.

Over the course of the next few weeks, I had the privilege of witnessing the interaction between the artists and these young women. Everyone told stories – some expressed anger or sadness at their circumstance. I heard about the condition of their homes and their schools. I heard the nonchalance in their voices when they talked about their babies, despite the fact that in my eyes, they were still babies themselves. I heard them express their dreams and aspirations, very few of them founded in any sort of reality. In the midst of hearing wishes for a professional boxing career or a multi-million dollar contract in the WNBA, one girl stated: "I want to graduate high school." Such a simplistic dream – one that was never even a consideration for me.

And then it dawned on me. Maybe I found it pretty easy to be an intelligent contributing member of society because my circumstances made it easy to do so. Maybe the fact that I lived in a neighborhood where it was safe to ride my bike – or the fact that I even had a bike – somehow contributed to the way I turned out. Perhaps my history with excellent teachers, professors, and school environments, enabled me to absorb the knowledge necessary to grow and mature. Maybe the fact that none of my friends were SHOT to death in oh-so-common gun violence allowed me to develop healthy, lasting relationships.

Ever since the GVRC program, I find myself stopping multiple times a week to reflect on my life and wondering about the lives of those young girls. How might I turn out if my circumstances were similar to those of the young women I met at GVRC? Would I feel empowered or capable enough to overcome those many, many obstacles? Would I, solely, be to blame for the choices I made on a daily basis? In all honesty, I am a product of my wholesome happy environment. And if I am a product of my environment, why would they not also be a product of theirs?

My change in perspective is not groundbreaking. I must admit that I am still living and working in my safely-guarded middle-class neighborhood. However, my outlook on social issues has been irrevocably altered. As a society, we are so quick to punish the wrong-doers: the gang-bangers, the drug users, the girls turning tricks for a living. I know because I was one of them, boasting a 'lock 'em up' mentality. But why do we forget to consider what lead people to make those choices?

GVRC taught me that young women in detainment are not monsters. They are not unavoidable bad seeds, destined to make up the future prison population of America. These young women are more often than not, a product of their crappy, underfunded, dilapidated environment (the one I previously refused to acknowledge). I used to be against funding special programs in low-income areas. I used to be hardened and closed to the reality that it's not only people in third-world countries facing "real problems" and devastating hardship. I no longer harbor those same feelings.

I cannot express enough gratitude to the leaders of this program, the workers at GVRC, and the young women I had the privilege of meeting. Thank you for allowing me to take part and observe. I am only one person, but my *perspective and my heart will forever be changed because of this experience. It goes without saying that I will never again question my "wealth."*

Internships often force students to rethink their existing values. It is, in many cases, their first experience coming into close contact with people who behave differently and have a different set of beliefs, especially with regard to right and wrong. Criminal Justice faculty often are concerned about the ability of students to cope in such vastly different environments. It is often necessary to do a fair amount of hand-holding to help students gain confidence and get through the experience. Though the internship experience often inspires students in important ways, rarely does it have the life-changing effects that it had on the interns participating in this program. Similar to Fehr (2006), the confidence of interns in this program increased, and "the otherness with which they regarded incarcerated people disappeared" (p. 280).

CHAPTER 7

Final Thoughts

The Buckham/GVRC Share Art Program is a work in progress. While initially conceptualized as a program pairing working visual artists with youth held in a county detention facility in Flint, Michigan, it has grown into a multidisciplinary arts program with a specialized gender-specific component.

Catering to the needs of youth in short term detention, staff and volunteers have constantly revised the program based upon the ideas and experiences of participants, detention staff, community stakeholders, and the artists themselves. The program has evolved from its roots as an outreach program created by a local arts organization to a multidisciplinary program involving professionals from the arts, academic, criminal justice, and judicial communities. It has received support and funding from local and national foundations, as well as a state-wide arts granting agency. The Project has mounted two exhibits and has been featured in local publications as well as juvenile law journals.

The Project established the first gender-specific program for young women involved in the criminal justice system in its area. The gender-specific Spoken Word poetry workshops evolved out of the observations, findings, and conclusions drawn from the original pilot program. Using the evidence obtained from the pilot project, as well as research on female criminality and gender-specific programming, project staff worked with the artists, academic researchers, and criminal justice professionals to develop a program designed to meet the needs of young female juvenile offenders.

According to all concerned (youth, GVRC staff, artists, criminal justice professionals), the Buckham/GVRC Share Art Project has been a success. The gender-specific Spoken Word Project has enabled young women to find their own voices and become tellers of their own stories. It has given them positive female role models and a safe space in which to explore and discuss issues relevant to them as females. Perhaps the biggest complaint is that the program does not do enough. All involved would like to see the development of additional classes in GVRC and classes for the participants in the community after their release.

7.1 INSTITUTIONAL CHALLENGES

Perhaps the greatest challenge encountered by the Project has been the short-term nature of the facility. As GVRC is a detention center and not a residential placement center, the average length of stay is 21 days. While many of the males are awaiting trials for adult offenses, the females are often detained for one to two weeks due to the less serious nature of their offending. As indicated in Chapter 4, the high turnover rate demanded that the instructors create workshops and activities that would be complete and self-sustaining in one session. This prevented them from working on longer-term writing and public speaking projects and assignments. It also made it difficult for them to give "homework" assignments, because new participants would be at a disadvantage.

The instability of the population also meant that each session had a different group dynamic. This caused many challenges for the instructors, because they had to spend additional time at the beginning of each session assessing the new participants. Often, young women would be brought to the workshop session almost immediately after admission into the detention center. Instructors had to be particularly sensitive to the needs of these newly detained, often traumatized, young women.

The wide variety in ages of the young women, their offenses, and their backgrounds proved to be challenging at times. Unlike residential treatment centers, which pre-screen residents for suitability to a particular program, no screening occurs before admission to GVRC. As a county detention facility, GVRC cannot pick and choose its residents. Young women are sent to GVRC either after court hearings or after-hours upon receiving telephone authorization from a court official. Many of the young women admitted to the detention center are suffering from withdrawal from drugs or alcohol, while others have not been properly maintained on psychotropic medications. The variety in the ages of the workshop participants was particularly challenging. For example, in one session their ages ranged from 12 to 16½. The age spread made it more difficult for the instructors to choose appropriate content and activities for the sessions, because the needs, abilities, and maturity of a twelve-year-old are far different from those of a sixteen-year-old.

Instructors had to be sensitive to the class, race, and cultural differences among the residents as well. As GVRC houses juveniles from the inner city of Flint, as well as the outlying suburbs and neighboring rural counties, the population of the female residents is usually quite diverse. The racial makeup of many of the sessions was fairly evenly divided between white, African American, and mixed race students. There was usually at least one young woman from a rural county and one from a more affluent suburb. The wide range of educational levels and linguistic styles had to be considered in planning Spoken Word workshops.

The nature of the offenses of the young women ranged from status offense probation violations to major felonies such as armed robbery and assault with intent to murder. Many of the young women were detained for domestic violence offenses in which they themselves had been victimized. For many, it was their first encounter with the juvenile justice system, while others had been locked up multiple times. The diversity of the young women, grouped together regardless of their offense or security level, was often quite challenging for the artists.

Changes in staffing at the detention center proved disruptive at times. The continuity of female staff members for the sessions was sometimes broken by schedule changes. As a result, staff members who were unfamiliar with the program and did not understand the dynamics of Spoken Word workshops were occasionally assigned to monitor the sessions. In these instances, the workshop environment seemed hostile, hindering the free expression of the participants.

Due to population shifts within GVRC, boys were placed in the girls' wing several times during the second and third sessions of programming. As noted previously, the mood of the young women changed when boys were on the wing. It took them longer to engage in the sessions, and caused some tension among the residents. During the third phase of programming, it also caused some of the young women to decide to participate in recreation activities with the boys instead of the female-only Spoken Word sessions.

Maintaining a male-free environment should be non-negotiable. The presence of even one male stifled the participants' willingness to share. At times, this was due to the young women's desire to flirt with the men in the room. But most importantly, the young women refused to open up and speak freely in the presence of males. This was especially apparent one evening when the female staff member was on vacation and a well-liked male staff member came into the room. Though he was clearly curious about the program and made his presence unobtrusive, the young women were completely uninvolved. Once the Program Director spoke to the supervisor, who asked him to leave the room, the mood immediately changed and the young women became involved. The artistic staff and the GVRC Administration were in agreement about the importance of having all-female staff in the room. The young women clearly benefitted from having strong female role models.

One problem mentioned by many of the young women was the absence of any similar programming after their release from GVRC. The need for a similar program in the community was echoed by criminal justice professionals (including judges, probation officers, and therapists) who worked with participants upon their release. They recognized the importance of this program for the young women and believed that it would continue to be beneficial upon their reentry into the community.

Unlike GVRC staff, some judges and probation officers were unfamiliar with the program. It would be helpful to acquaint them with the work of the program and how it affects many of the girls. Those professionals who are familiar with the program have been supportive, but many professionals are unaware of its existence. A forum where those familiar with the program can share their experiences and encourage others to follow suit would be quite useful. With greater support within the criminal justice community, a more stable source of funding and additional funding to develop a post-release program will be possible.

7.2 ARTISTIC CHALLENGES

As mentioned in Chapter 3, the restrictions on language and expression were initially seen by the artist/instructors as contradictory to the nature and purpose of Spoken Word. While they were able to accommodate the sessions to fit within the parameters of the institution, the rule prohibiting discussion of the residents' offenses often inhibited the cathartic process of the young women's writing. As the nature of girls' offending is generally tied to their family and life histories (see discussion on gendered pathways in Chapter 2), it was often difficult to separate the two, particularly in cases involving domestic assault on a parent. In order for the young women to become the "Active I" in their own lives and tell their story in their own words, inclusion of information about their offenses would make the process more meaningful.

With the introduction of the gender-specific programming, the instructors sometimes lost sight of their roles as artists and teachers and instead look at themselves as facilitators or therapists. With the introduction of gender-pertinent issues, the sessions became more internally focused, at times causing the workshops to resemble group therapy sessions rather than poetry workshops. At these times the focus of the class strayed from writing and some of the creativity of the program was lost or stifled. The artists wanted to maintain a safe place where the young women could express themselves freely and not feel shut down. While this was extremely important, the instructors needed to remain in control of the dynamics of the workshop. In order to accomplish this, the artist/instructors, project coordinator, and interns had to constantly work together to maintain a balanced atmosphere that would encourage the release of feelings and emotions through artistic expression. This required the instructors and interns to spend more time working individually with each of the young women and assist them in using their writing creatively to express their innermost thoughts.

7.3 RECOMMENDATIONS

1. *Collaboration between the Artists, the Arts Organization, the Detention Administration, and Staff is necessary.* A close working relationship between all involved is vital. Collaboration between both agencies' administrations and the artists is very important. Staff should be included whenever possible. Continuous open communication among all involved in the development of the program is also vital. At the very least, there should be monthly meetings which include the Program Director and representatives from the Arts Organization and the facility.
2. *A Program Director who has a working knowledge about the Criminal Justice System and the Arts Organization must be identified.* There should be one identifiable Program Director who is involved with both the arts and the criminal justice system. This individual should be copied on all communications regarding the program. Any issues that need resolution must be handled by the Program Director.
3. *When selecting artists, it is necessary to keep in mind their craft and their effectiveness with youth.* Careful selection of artists/teachers

should have high priority so that the project brings to the youth experienced artists who can teach. Communication between the participants and artists is crucial.

4. *Artists should be long-standing residents of the community so that they fully understand the community's culture and can serve as adult role models.* It is important that artists come from the local community so that they fully understand the needs and issues of the youth involved. It is important that the artists be able to identify with the youth and show a deep understanding of the local culture and associated problems.

5. *The artistic team should be multidisciplinary, multi-age, and multicultural.* It is imperative that the Project maintain its multidisciplinary nature so that issues can be examined from an artistic and social science perspective. The arts staff employed in the Project ranged in age from 23–60. This gave the young women a chance to observe a wide variety of "strong" women.

6. *Programs for young women must be "male-free."* The presence of even one male in the room completely changes the dynamics in the room. Having a "male-free" environment allows the women to relate to one another as women in a safe environment.

7. *Programs need to incorporate gender-responsive and culturally relevant programming.* Since it is clear that the needs of male and female offenders differ, programs should focus on the specific needs of young women. The principles of gender-specific programming should provide the framework for the program.

8. *It is important that artists have little knowledge of the youths' offenses and background; however, it is important that training include a basic understanding of the court process, the rules of the facility, and the principles of gender-specific programming.* Although it is important that staff make the artists aware of any potential issues, the less the artists know about the specifics of the youth's offenses and backgrounds, the less likely they are to treat any individual differently.

9. *It is necessary to have one person designated to take careful notes during each session in order to document the lesson as well as moods and interactions among the participants and staff.* Because the sessions are often very emotional, the artists sometimes are unable to separate the lesson from the emotions conveyed. Therefore, having clear documentation of what occurs during each session allows the staff to assess the impact of any given lesson.

10. *Staff should aim for a program that stresses both the artistic/creative component while focusing on issues that are important to young women.* The program should not be viewed as a "therapy" program, but as a chance to encourage the youth's creativity. Encouraging the use of writing and speaking to express their emotions builds skills and confidence.

11. *Ongoing observations and evaluations are needed to make changes and refinements in the program.* The program should be flexible to adapt lessons according to the population. Regularly examining "what works" and making changes accordingly is necessary to ensure a quality program.

12. *Funding should include money for evaluation in order to determine if the program has an effect on reducing participants' offending behavior.* Because the program began simply as a means of introducing art to an under-served population, the potential of the program to reduce recidivism has not been examined. However, we recognize the importance of assessing the program's impact on recidivism and intend to request funding for that purpose in future grant proposals.

BIBLIOGRAPHY

REFERENCES

Blanchette, K., & Taylor, K. N. (2009). Reintegration of female offenders: perspectives on "What Works". *Corrections Today*, 60–63.

Bloom, B., Owen, B., & Covington, S. (2008). *Gender-responsive strategies for women offenders: A summary of "Research, practice, and guiding principles for women offenders"*. Washington, D.C: National Institute of Corrections. NIC accession no. 020418.

Bloom, B., Owen, B., Deschenes, E. P., & Rosenbaum, J. (2002). Developing gender-specific services for delinquency prevention: understanding risk and resiliency. In R. Muraskin (Ed.), *It's a crime: Women and justice* (3rd ed., pp. 792–819). New York: Prentice Hall.

Bloom, B. E., & Covington, S. S. (1998, November 11–14). *Gender-specific programming for female offenders: What is it and why is it important? Paper presented at the 50th Annual Meeting of the American Society of Criminology*, Washington, D.C.

Brown Morton, J. (2007). Providing gender-responsive services for women and girls. *Corrections Today*, *6*, 12.

Calabrese, R. L., & Adams, J. (1990). Alienation: a cause of juvenile delinquency. *Journal of Adolescence*, *25*(98), 435–440.

Chesney-Lind, M., & Irwin, K. (2008). *Beyond bad girls: Gender, violence and hype*. New York: Routledge.

Chesney-Lind, M., Morash, M., & Stevens, T. (2008). Girls' troubles, girls' delinquency, and gender responsive programming: a review. *The Australian and New Zealand Journal of Criminology*, *41*(1), 162–189.

Emerson, E., & Shelton, D. (2001). Using creative arts to build coping skills to reduce domestic violence in the lives of female juvenile offenders. *Issues in Mental Health Nursing*, *22*, 181–195.

Ezell, M., & Levy, M. (2003). An evaluation of an arts program for incarcerated juvenile offenders. *Journal of Correctional Education*, *54*(3), 108–114.

Fehr, D. E. (2006). How to draw a heart: teaching art to incarcerated youth. *The Journal of Social Theory in Art Education*, *26*, 258–281.

Goodkind, S. (2005). Gender-specific services in the juvenile justice system: a critical examination. *Affilia*, *2*(1), 52–70.

Hillman, G. (2006). *Arts Programs for Juvenile Offenders in Detention and Corrections: A Guide to Promising Practices*. Washington, DC: Office of Juvenile Justice and Delinquency Prevention.

Hillman, G. (1993). Arts programs for juvenile offenders in Texas. *Texas Recreation and Park Society*, 6–7.

Jones Hubbard, D., & Matthews, B. (2008). Reconciling the differences between the "Gender-Responsive" and the "What Works" literatures to improve services for girls. *Crime & Delinquency*, *54*(2), 225–258.

Lazzari, M. M., Amundson, K. A., & Jackson, R. L. (2005). "We are more than jailbirds": an arts program for incarcerated young women. *Affilia*, *20*(2), 169–185.

Matthews, B., & Jones Hubbard, D. (2008). Moving ahead: five essential elements for working effectively with girls. *Journal of Criminal Justice*, *36*, 494–502.

Mullen, C. A. (1999). Reaching inside out: arts-based educational programming for incarcerated women. *Studies in Art Education, 40*(2), 143–161.

NCCD Center for Girls and Young Women. (2009, February). *Getting the facts straight about girls in the juvenile justice system. Retrieved from* <http://www.nccdglobal.org/sites/default/files/publication_pdf/fact-sheet-girls-in-juvenile-justice.pdf>.

Odgers, C. L., Moretti, M. M., & Dickon Reppucci, N. (2005). Examining the science and practice of violence risk assessment with female adolescents. *Law and Human Behavior, 29*(1), 7–27.

Oesterreich, H. A., & McNie Flores, S. (2009). Learning to c: visual arts education as strengths based practice in juvenile correctional facilities. *The Journal of Correctional Education, 60*(2), 146–162.

Persons, R. W. (2009). Art therapy with serious juvenile offenders. *International Journal of Offender Therapy and Comparative Criminology, 53*(4), 433–453.

Quraishi, F. (2012). Enhancing mental health advocacy for girls in the juvenile justice system. *Youth Law News, 31*, 4.

Ross, R. R., Fabiano, E., & Ross, R. (1988). (Re)Habilitation through education: a cognitive model for corrections. *Journal of Correctional Education, 39*(2), 44–47.

Salzman, M. (2003). *True notebooks: A writer's year at Juvenile Hall.* New York: Vintage Books.

Sanger, D., Maag, J. W., & Spilker, A. (2006). Communication and behavioral considerations in planning programs for female juvenile delinquents. *The Journal of Correctional Education, 57*(2), 108–125.

Smeijsters, H., Kil, J., Kurstjens, H., Welten, J., Welten, J., & Willemars, G. (2011). Arts therapies for young offenders in secure care—A practice-based research. *The Arts in Psychotherapy, 38*, 41–51.

Strom, K. J., Warner, T. D., Tichavsky, L., & Zahn, M. A. (2010). Policing juveniles: domestic violence arrest policies, gender, and police response to child-parent violence. *Crime & Delinquency, 20*(10), 1–24.

Watson, L., & Edelman, P. (2013). Improving the juvenile justice system for girls: lessons from the states. *Georgetown Journal of Law & Public Policy, 20*, 215–268.

Wu, L. (2010, June). *Why do we need gender-responsive assessments, programs and services for justice-involved girls? Retrieved from* <http://www.prisonlaw.com/pdfs/WhyGirls.pdf>.

CPSIA information can be obtained at www.ICGtesting.com
Printed in the USA
BVOW11s0608270114

342979BV00010B/87/P